GALATIANS

A New Testament Commentary

Bob Yandian

Isa 33:6

All bolded and, unless otherwise indicated, block scripture quotations are from the *New King James Version* of the Bible ®. Copyright © 1982 by Thomas Nelson. Used by permission. All rights reserved.

All other scripture quotations, unless otherwise noted, are from the *King James Version* of the Bible.

Scripture quotations from the following versions are used by permission:

New American Standard Bible, © 1960, 1962, 1968, 1971, 1973, 1975, 1977 by The Lockman Foundation.

Holy Bible, *New International Version*, © 1973, 1978, 1984 by the International Bible Society.

The Living Bible, © 1971 by Tyndale House Publishers, Wheaton, Illinois.

Galatians: A New Testament Commentary

ISBN: 978-68031-084-9
© 2016 by Bob Yandian
Bob Yandian Ministries
PO Box 55236
Tulsa, OK 74155
www.bobyandian.com

Published by Harrison House Publishers
Tulsa, OK 74155
www.harrisonhouse.com

21 20 19 18   10 9 8 7 6 5 4 3 2

All rights reserved under International Copyright Law. Contents and/or cover may not be reproduced in whole or in part in any form without the express written consent of the publisher.

Printed in the United States of America.

Table of Contents

GALATIANS

VERSE BY VERSE COMMENTARY

The personal study notes of BOB YANDIAN

Introduction

My heart echoes a statement Peter made in his last epistle:

For this reason I will not be negligent to remind you always of these things, though you know and are established in the present truth.

2 Peter 1:12

The "for this reason" was to build on his previous statement — Peter's desire for all believers not just to get to heaven, but to have an abundant entrance into heaven. A working knowledge and practice of the Word of God is necessary for an abundant entrance, which is marked by rewards and rulership.

In order to establish that abundant entrance, Peter taught believers what they should know again and again, "though you know them." What was taught them was the present truth. The present truth is what was being written in the day of the apostles Peter, Paul, John, and James.

This present truth is what believers still need to be gloriously saved. The Old Testament is to be studied in the light of the New Testament epistles. The four gospels are to be studied in the light of the New Testament epistles. Not only should every Christian know the epistles, they should be established in them.

This is why I have written this series of books, verse-by-verse teachings on the epistles of Paul, Peter, John, and James. This is truly meat for our time period, our dispensation: the church age.

Bob Yandian
Author

Galatians Overview

Galatians is an exciting book. In it, the apostle Paul laid down a foundation of what every Christian needs to guard against. It's the most subtle trap believers can fall into: the trap of legalism.

Now when legalism is mentioned, most Christians automatically think of the Ten Commandments or the Mosaic law. But legalism involves much more than these two obvious examples. It is much more subtle than that, much less evident and therefore much more dangerous.

To the Jews of Paul's day, legalism was primarily an overemphasis on the observance of Jewish law which blinded them to the gospel of salvation by grace. To the modern-day Christian, legalism is more an attitude than an act, which makes it all the more difficult to detect and avoid. We may not even be aware that we are guilty of it. Because it is so insidious, we have unsuspectingly allowed this attitude to creep into virtually every facet of our daily Christian lives. In this study we will be defining legalism and examining its effect upon us as Christians. We will see how it has come to exert an influence upon everything in our church life from water baptism to personal witnessing. We will also consider the dangers of legalism and discuss ways to overcome this most subtle of Satan's attack upon the church of Jesus Christ.

In essence, the book of Galatians is a declaration of faith and faith alone. Faith for salvation and faith for spirituality. This faith is not based on any effort or action or observance on our part, but is founded solely and entirely upon the grace of God. In fact, Galatians could be called a manifesto of grace.

Before we actually begin our study of this powerful book, let's review a moment. Exactly who were the Galatians to whom Paul addressed this letter? If you are familiar with New Testament history, you will remember that Galatia was an area northwest of Israel that had been settled by the Gauls in the third century. It became a Roman province in 25 B.C., some years before Paul began his missionary journeys to the region. The Galatians were descendants of barbaric tribes that had infiltrated the Roman Empire. These tribes were all branches of the Celts who later settled Ireland, Scotland, and Wales. The Galatians are distant cousins of the modern-day Irish.

In his opening salutation, Paul directed his remarks to the churches of Galatia. Notice, "churches" is plural. Galatians is the only one of Paul's epistles directed to more than one church. Ephesians was written to the church in Ephesus; Philippians addressed the church in Philippi. However, Galatians was sent to the churches of Galatia, because Galatia is not a city but a province.

There were four major cities in the province of Galatia: Antioch, Iconium, Derbe, and Lystra. The city of Lystra should be familiar to us because that's where, on his first missionary journey, Paul was nearly stoned to death. But God restored him, and he was able to go back into the city to preach to the people. (You can read about this event in Acts 14.)

In the book of Galatians, we will be considering several basic themes: the Abrahamic covenant, the blessing of Abraham, redemption from the curse of the law, the fruit of the Spirit versus works of the flesh, and several others. As we study, we will be referring back to the Old Testament where we will learn about Abraham, Sarah, Hagar, Isaac, and Ishmael. From there we will go to the New Testament to follow Paul's missionary journey to Galatia. We will talk about Paul's thorn in the flesh and consider what it might have been. We will see how his message was always the same: faith for salvation and faith for spirituality. We will see how, because of his message, Paul was hounded and harassed everywhere he went by legalistic Judaizers with their insistence that organized religion was the only means to salvation. Through all this, our attention will be fixed upon one central truth: the grace of God poured out at Calvary, freeing us from all self-striving so we may live truly Spirit-filled, fruitful lives of freedom and joy.

In chapter 1 of Galatians, we will read Paul's testimony of his call to the ministry. We will see how he stressed that it was the Lord Himself who called, commissioned, and ordained him to carry the good news of salvation by grace to the Gentiles. We will see that Paul's knowledge of this truth came not from man or from men, but directly from God through personal revelation.

Later on, in chapter 2 of Galatians, we will see how Paul met some of his enemies among the religious people of his day and how he dealt with them, utterly defeating them with the message of faith. We will also see how, although afraid to oppose him face-to-face, these enemies of the gospel worked against what Paul was doing by sneaking in behind him to undermine what he had begun in the establishment of new churches. They would plant seeds of doubt in Paul's followers, insinuating that he was not a true apostle of the Lord Jesus Christ, casting aspersions upon his character and his message, laying heavy legalistic burdens upon the new believers, upon those who were not even Jews and thus never subject to Jewish law.

Also in chapter 2, Paul recounted two stories: the first story will be that of the Jerusalem incident in which he gave us an example of an attempt to receive salvation by works; the second story is that of the Antioch incident, which illustrates the false concept of spirituality by works. The end of the chapter deals with his famous confrontation before the whole church at Antioch in which he openly rebuked Peter for becoming involved in legalism.

Then in chapter 3, we will see how Paul used these two incidents to set up the Galatians for the rebuke he levels against them for falling into legalism because of their lack of understanding of grace.

In chapter 4, Paul took the example of Abraham and his offspring to illustrate this faith principle which he further developed in chapter 5 using Abraham's two wives and sons to contrast works of the flesh with the fruit of the Spirit.

Finally in chapter 6, we will see how Paul concluded his remarks by examining the question of how a person can become spiritual again after having been carnally-minded for so long.

In its overall outline, the book of Galatians parallels the book of Ephesians. Both address the subject of grace versus legalism. But where Ephesians emphasizes the positive side, Galatians stresses the negative aspect of this conflict. Not that the book itself is negative; however in Ephesians, Paul laid more emphasis on how wonderful it was to understand grace, whereas in Galatians he points out the stupidity of falling for legalism.

As we approach this book, we must remember that Paul learned through written letters what had been happening in the churches in Galatia during his absence following his first missionary journey there. He was so disturbed about these events that he was moved to write this letter. Note that Paul was not coming to Galatia in person to straighten things out. He was simply writing to these churches to confront them with their foolishness in turning back to "dead works" after having once received the glorious gospel of grace.

In our study we will see that this is not a sweet letter. Paul was obviously angry with these people and made no attempt to hide his anger. We get the distinct impression that he must have been pounding on the table as he wrote these words of rebuke. He did not mince words with the Galatians whom he referred to as "foolish." (A more accurate term would be "stupid"! We will examine some translations other than the *New King James Version* to show that this was indeed the tone of Paul's message to these people.)

The primary problem was that the Galatians who had entered their spiritual walk by faith, were now attempting to complete that walk by adhering to Jewish law. This happened because they began to listen to the legalistic Judaizers, many of whom were truly born again, yet insisted that compliance with the strict codes of Judaism applied equally to Gentile Christians as well as to Jews. The Galatians who had embraced the message of Christ were now trying to combine the message of grace with the observance of Jewish law. In essence, they were trying to straddle the fence between legalism and grace, to live by the precepts of the New Testament while adhering to the rules and regulations of the Old. Paul made it abundantly clear that such a walk was not only impossible, it was a denial of the atonement and an abomination in the sight of God.

The Galatians simply did not have a proper understanding of the Old and New Testaments. They did not realize that the old covenant was not abolished and fulfilled by the birth, death, and resurrection of the Messiah. The old covenant is still to be studied and taught, but it is not to be observed. The Old Testament merely points to the coming of the Lord Jesus Christ who perfectly and completely fulfilled all the righteous demands of the law for all those who will accept that fulfillment by faith. Once Christ made the supreme sacrifice for sin, no other sacrifice was necessary. Old things passed away; all things became new. The shadow gave way to the reality.

This led to questions like circumcision — which is one of the major topics of the book of Galatians — because it represents the whole gamut of rules and regulations embodied in the old covenant. Paul stressed to the Galatians that while circumcision is fine for health reasons, it no longer has any spiritual value.

This letter was delivered to Galatia where it was to be passed around among the four churches in Antioch, Iconium, Derbe, and Lystra. Let's begin our study of this, the most scathing accusation Paul ever leveled against religion, allowing it to set us free from the law of sin and death, that we may discover in it the fullness of life in the Spirit.

1:1 Apostleship

I. Paul, an Apostle

1:1 ¶ Paul, an apostle (not from men nor through man, but through Jesus Christ and God the Father who raised Him from the dead),

In this opening verse, Paul immediately identifies himself as the author of this book. The word "Paul" in Greek is *Paulus*, meaning little. This seems to be descriptive of the man because Christian tradition has it that Paul was not a man of great physical stature. He was short. In the natural realm, Paul considered himself small. But we know that if a person is small in his own eyes, God considers him great in the spiritual realm.

So many Christians today are boasting of how they are the righteousness of God in Christ Jesus, which is scripturally true, but is nothing to get puffed up in pride about. Unless a person realizes he is nothing in the natural realm, he will be nothing in the spiritual realm either. God looks upon the heart, and no heart is great that boasts of its greatness. It is the inner man that is important, not the outer man. I like the expression, "I'm bigger on the inside than I am on the outside." That's true. Since Jesus lives inside us, we believers are bigger within than without. Even when this outer shell has crumbled into dust, the inner man will keep on living with the Lord Jesus forever and ever.

Paul makes his strongest claim to his calling, noting that he is an apostle not of men (plural), neither by man (singular), "but though Jesus Christ, and God the Father, who raised him from the dead."

Paul is actually saying, "I am an apostle. No group of men chose me, and no individual man chose me. I was ordained to this position by Jesus Christ and by God the Father." Paul stresses two negative aspects of his calling, and one positive aspect of it. He was not appointed by men, not by a man, but by the Lord Himself.

What is an apostle? The English word "apostle" is actually a transliteration of the Greek word *apostolos*, just as the English word "baptize" is a transliteration of the Greek word *baptizo*, meaning to immerse or dip in water. Since we had no word in English for this concept, the original translators simply adopted the Greek word into English. So it was with apostle. Since

English had no real equivalent of the word *apostolos*, the translators transliterated it, almost letter for letter, into our language.

What does "apostle" actually mean? *Strong's Concordance* defines it as "a delegate; spec. an ambassador of the gospel; officially a commissioner of Christ [apostle] (with miraculous powers): apostle, messenger, he that is sent."

Ephesians 4:11 lists the office of apostle as one of the fivefold ministry gifts given to the church by the Lord Jesus Christ and God the Father. To understand this office more fully, here are several aspects of apostleship.

II. Apostleship

A. First Office Placed into the Church of Jesus Christ

As we have seen, the Greek word *apostolos* implies a sent one. If we trace the word back even further into history, we learn it came from the ancient Phoenician language and it referred to the highest ranking officer in the Phoenician navy (the equivalent of our English word "admiral"). Does this have any significance for us today? Although the apostle does not outrank other ministers on a scale of authority, rank does have significance in the modern church. In 1 Corinthians 12:28 Paul writes: "And God hath set some in the church, first apostles, secondarily prophets, thirdly teachers, after that miracles, then gifts of healings, helps, governments, diversities of tongues." Notice that phrase "first apostles."

Although an apostle may have authority over a church he established and possibly left, "first apostles" does not indicate rank over other ministry gifts; it indicates when the office of the apostle was placed in the body of Christ. After the day of Pentecost, the first office given to the church was apostle. Through the remainder of the book of Acts, other offices came into being as evangelism took place and local churches were raised up. The next office given after the apostle was the prophet. The third was the teacher, and so on with the remaining ministries.

This can be seen in the first area of conflict within the church in Acts 6. The problem associated with the neglect of widows was brought before the Twelve. The church leadership consisted of apostles only, those who followed Jesus Himself. By the time of the sending out of the apostles to evangelize in Acts 13, they are brought before the church leadership made up of prophets and teachers (13:1). In Acts 14, the first churches are established and pastors are ordained, called elders (14:23).

It is still the same today. Apostles may be the first to enter a city where there is little or no spiritual activity. They evangelize and disciple believers until a church is established. They then help raise up church leadership and finally leave to begin the process again in another city or country.

B. Ministry Gift Given by Jesus Christ and God the Father

In 1 Corinthians 12:28, notice who sets these offices in the church: "And *God* has appointed these in the church" (emphasis added). Bob Yandian did not set Bob Yandian in the office of pastor. God the Father placed me there. If you have a calling on your life to one of the fivefold ministry offices, no man placed that calling on you; God placed it. If God has called you, He will see to it that you have ample opportunity to fulfill that calling. All you have to do is stand firm and allow Him to fulfill it through you. Your part is to pray and stay in the Word. God will develop the gift. It's not up to you to promote yourself; your task is simply to prove yourself faithful. God will see to the rest.

In Ephesians 4:11 we find this statement: "And He Himself gave some to be apostles, some prophets, some evangelists, and some pastors and teachers." Who is it that "gave some"? Jesus Christ. How do we know this? Four verses back, we read these words: "But unto every one of us is given grace according to the measure of the gift of Christ" (v. 7). The apostle is a gift given to (set in) the church through the cooperation of Jesus Christ and God the Father.

When Paul asserts he was an apostle (one of highest rank) — chosen and commissioned to ministry; not by men, nor by man, but by Jesus Christ and God the Father — he was claiming divine ordination (which is the case of every true apostle, prophet, evangelist, pastor, and teacher). When Paul made reference to the fact that he was divinely ordained rather than ordained by men, he was probably referring to the Jewish council in Jerusalem. The reason he stressed this point was because his credentials and his authority to minister as an apostle of Jesus Christ were called into question by the legalistic Judaizers. They wanted to know, "Who is this Paul?"

They were quick to point out he had no papers showing he had been certified as an apostle by the Jerusalem council. This, of course, was true because Paul argued apostleship is not of men, but of God. These detractors also said Peter or one of the other disciples had not laid hands on Paul and commissioned him as an apostle. This was also true because, again, Paul insisted apostleship is not conferred by any individual man but by the Lord.

This is an important truth that deserves our attention. No group of men and no one individual passes on the spiritual gifts of the fivefold ministry. These come directly from God. There are other offices in the Word of God that can be given by men by the laying on of hands (cf. Acts 14:23, Titus 1:5) No one can make himself an apostle, prophet, evangelist, pastor, or teacher, and no one can choose and appoint another person to any one of these offices. The right and power of appointment to the fivefold ministry rests solely and exclusively with God the Father and Jesus Christ.

Neither can these ministry gifts be received by faith. Now I am a strong believer in the power of personal faith. I believe in it wholeheartedly. However, there are some things that simply cannot be received by faith, by simply believing and confessing you have them. One of these things is appointment to the fivefold ministry. No one can become a minister of the gospel of Jesus Christ by simply proclaiming, "By faith I believe I am an apostle (prophet, evangelist, pastor, teacher)." That will not work. This appointment is a gift divinely and sovereignly conferred upon a person by God the Father and the Lord Jesus Christ.

Apostleship is not conferred by human hands or received through personal faith, nor is it determined by talent; rather, it is strictly a matter of God's grace.

A talent is a natural human ability innate within the individual who possesses it. In other words, talent is something you are born with. All of us have one or more inborn natural talents. Some of us are musically gifted, others have great artistic or creative talent, and others are endowed with a natural ability to learn languages easily. But none of these natural gifts have anything to do with the ministry gifts. These are bestowed upon individuals by God without regard to human ability.

Some people think just because they can play a guitar, they are called into the music ministry. Others think because they have some speaking ability, they are called to be a pastor or an evangelist. Still others mistake intellectual capacity as a call to become a teacher of the Word of God. That is a mistake. Apostleship, as well as any other ministry office, is not a matter of talent but of divine appointment.

C. Early Apostleship Not the Same As Apostleship to the Church

Apostles to the church were not appointed until after the resurrection of the Lord Jesus Christ. This is a vitally important point.

In Ephesians we read:

> 7 But to each one of us grace was given according to the mea-
> sure of Christ's gift. 8 Therefore He says:
>
> "*When He ascended on high,*
> *He led captivity captive,*
> *And gave gifts to men.*"
>
> 9 (Now this, "He ascended"—what does it mean but that He also
> first descended into the lower parts of the earth? 10 He who de-
> scended is also the One who ascended far above all the heavens,
> that He might fill all things.)11 And He Himself gave some to
> be apostles, some prophets, some evangelists, and some pastors
> and teachers, —Ephesians 4:7–11

Since this passage makes it clear that Christ ordained and established the
fivefold ministry after His resurrection from the dead and His ascension
into heaven, it is obvious there is a difference between the apostles chosen and appointed in the four gospels (Matthew, Mark, Luke, and John)
before Christ's ascension and those apostles given to the church after He
had returned to the right hand of His Father in heaven. This is even more
evident when we consider that the church of Jesus Christ did not even
come into existence until after the resurrection and ascension of our Lord.
The fivefold ministry was initiated with the beginning of the church age,
which did not begin with the gospel of Matthew but rather in the book of
Acts.

Let's consider this point for a moment. In Matthew 10:1–6, we read about
Jesus' commissioning His disciples for ministry:

> 1 And when He had called His twelve disciples to Him, He gave
> them power over unclean spirits, to cast them out, and to heal
> all kinds of sickness and all kinds of disease. 2 Now the names
> of the twelve apostles are these: first, Simon, who is called Peter,
> and Andrew his brother; James the son of Zebedee, and John his
> brother; 3 Philip and Bartholomew; Thomas and Matthew the tax
> collector; James the son of Alphaeus, and Lebbaeus, whose sur-
> name was Thaddaeus; 4 Simon the Cananite, and Judas Iscariot,

who also betrayed Him. 5 These twelve Jesus sent out and commanded them, saying: "Do not go into the way of the Gentiles, and do not enter a city of the Samaritans. 6 But go rather to the lost sheep of the house of Israel. —Matthew 10:1–6

Notice in verse 1, these twelve men are referred to as disciples, whereas in verse 2, they are called apostles. Are these apostles the same as the apostles we read about in the epistles of Paul? In verses 5 and 6, we see that Jesus sent these men to the Jews only. They were specifically commanded not to minister to Gentiles or Samaritans. That brings up an interesting question: Is the church of Jesus Christ made up only of Jews? No, of course not. It's made up of both Jews and Gentiles.

It seems quite clear there is a difference between those called apostles in the four gospels and those divinely appointed as apostles after the establishment of the church of Jesus Christ. It is important we understand this difference. Although most of the twelve disciples did go on to become true apostles after the resurrection of the Lord Jesus, their ministries totally changed after the day of Pentecost when the church came into existence. God was no longer dealing with one nation. He now dealt with all nations through the church, which is the body of Christ.

When Paul talked in Ephesians about the apostleship, he was not referring to the ministry of the twelve disciples or to that of the seventy sent out in Luke 10. He was speaking specifically of those chosen and ordained by God the Father and the Lord Jesus Christ to go and minister the gospel throughout the whole world. He was speaking of those divinely appointed to the fivefold ministry of the church.

D. Still Exists Today

Some people claim the day of miracles has ceased because the day of the apostles has passed. Is that true? No, not in either case. Miracles have not ceased because the day of the apostles has not passed.

"Do you mean to say there are apostles today?"

Yes, I do.

Some churches preach that when the original apostles died, miracles and tongues and prophecy died with them. They say these gifts were given by Jesus to get the church started, but once it began, those things were no longer needed and no longer provided.

But 1 Corinthians 12:28 says, "And God hath set some in the church, first apostles, secondarily prophets, thirdly teachers, after that miracles, then gifts of healings, helps, governments, diversities of tongues." Does the church still exist today? Well, if God has set some in the church to be apostles and the church is still alive and functioning, what makes us think these apostles are not still alive and functioning as well? If teaching and helps and government have not ceased (and what church do you know of that does not teach, help, and govern its members?), then why should we believe prophecy, miracles, healings, or tongues would have ceased? To the extent that any of these things have ceased, it is not because God has withdrawn them, but because churches are simply not practicing them!

How can we say apostles and prophets have disappeared when we still have evangelists, pastors, and teachers in our churches? Where in the Bible does it say any of these positions have been taken out of the church? You won't find such a scripture because it just doesn't exist. Apostleship is as much a part of the New Testament churches today as it was at the time Paul wrote this letter to the churches in Galatia.

Some people tell me they don't know any apostles today, but they do. We just don't call them by that name. Today they are known as missionaries, the sent ones. These are the ones who go into all the world to preach the good news, win converts to the Lord Jesus Christ, establish churches, train pastors, and then move on to the next place of service. That's why we should give our prayer and financial support to our missionaries. The call to the mission field is a high calling of God upon a person's life. Apostles are missionaries, but all missionaries are not apostles. Many are called to help win the lost or to aid in ministry on foreign fields but not to establish churches throughout a country. The term missionary is a broad; we use it to identify those called to foreign mission work. Apostle is a specific calling on an individual by God the Father and the Lord Jesus Christ.

Whether you and I are called to that high office or not, we can do our part in that ministry through our prayers and financial support of those who do go forth to fulfill God's high calling on their lives.

There are still apostles today. They are the missionaries, those (like the apostle Paul) whose lives are devoted to carrying the gospel to every nation. The only difference between today's apostles and those of Paul's day is modern-day apostles do not write Scripture. Today the written Word of God is complete. With the recording of the Revelation of Jesus Christ given to John on the Isle of Patmos, the Word was completed, but the ministry gift of apostleship still continues today. It will go on until the return of our Lord Jesus to this earth to gather His own unto Himself at the end of the church age.

E. Always Accompanied by Spiritual Gifts

The office of apostle carries with it spiritual gifts. The same holds true of any one of the other fivefold ministries. If a person is called to be a teacher of the Word of God, he has been endowed with spiritual gifts to accomplish that work. The same holds true for the apostle, evangelist, prophet, and pastor. Each one called to fulfill an office of the fivefold ministry receives the spiritual endowments necessary to equip him or her for that assigned task.

In Romans 11:29 we read, "For the gifts and calling of God are without repentance." Gifts and calling go hand in hand. If you have been called by God to a particular ministry, then you have been equipped by Him with the spiritual gifts necessary to carry out that ministry.

Notice the source of the gifts is God. Notice also the source of the callings: God. Therefore, if you know you are called by the Lord, don't worry about your ability (or lack of ability) to fulfill that call. The gifts to fulfill the office come with the call.

Some people say to me, "Yes, that's easy for you to say; you've been a pastor for a long time. But I'm just beginning to minister. I'm not sure the gifts will operate through me if I launch out in my ministry." I tell them, "Don't worry about it. If you have been called by God, you have the gifts within you. If you will just stay in faith, those gifts will begin to operate in God's time."

Although you have certain spiritual gifts, you can't pick and choose which you want to work through you. You can't say, "Well, I believe I'll allow the gift of miracles to work through me, but I don't want the gift of tongues." That won't work. Neither can you believe for any certain gift you think you might like to have. The Bible says the Holy Spirit divides "to every man severally as he will" (1 Corinthians 12:11). It does not say you can pick and choose which ones you would like to receive and refuse the others. The Lord gives you the gifts of the Spirit that will best enhance the office in which you stand. Just as God is sovereign in choosing the office for you, He is sovereign in choosing the gifts you will operate in. The gifts and callings of God are without repentance.

The Word teaches us to covet earnestly the best gifts (1 Corinthians 12:31).However, you are not to choose the gifts, but to seek earnestly for the best gifts, which will cause your office to come to its maximum effectiveness. Seek only those gifts that will accomplish God's calling upon your life. You have every reason to desire them and every right to receive them. They come with the call.

F. Conferred by God, Not Man

As we have noted, in Galatians 1:1, Paul claims he was appointed an apostle by God the Father and the Lord Jesus Christ, not by man or men. That statement always raises the question, "But what about Matthias?" To answer that question, let's look at the story as found in Acts 1.

Just prior to His ascension into heaven, the Lord Jesus spoke to His disciples who were gathered together with Him on the Mount of Olives. He instructed them to wait in Jerusalem until they had received the gift He would pour out on them, the gift of the Holy Spirit. He told them with that gift of the Holy Spirit, they would receive power to be His witnesseses "both in Jerusalem, and in all Judaea, and in Samaria, and unto the uttermost part of the earth" (v. 8).

After speaking these things to them, the Lord was taken up out of their sight. While they were still standing there in amazement and wonder, two angels appeared to them and said, "Ye men of Galilee, why stand ye gazing up into heaven? This same Jesus, which is taken up from you into heaven, shall so come in like manner as ye have seen him go into heaven" (v. 11). The disciples returned to Jerusalem to wait for the promise of the coming Holy Spirit.

It was while they were praying and waiting for the Holy Spirit to be poured out upon them that Peter got the idea of filling the vacancy left by the betrayal and death of Judas Iscariot:

> 15 And in those days Peter stood up in the midst of the disciples (altogether the number of names was about a hundred and twenty), and said, 16 "Men and brethren, this Scripture had to be fulfilled, which the Holy Spirit spoke before by the mouth of David concerning Judas, who became a guide to those who arrested Jesus; 17 for he was numbered with us and obtained a part in this ministry." 18 (Now this man purchased a field with the wages of iniquity; and falling headlong, he burst open in the middle and all his entrails gushed out. 19 And it became known to all those dwelling in Jerusalem; so that field is called in their own language, *Akel Dama*, that is, Field of Blood.) 20 "For it is written in the Book of Psalms:

> 'Let his dwelling place be desolate,
> And let no one live in it';

and,

> 'Let another take his office.'

21 "Therefore, of these men who have accompanied us all the time that the Lord Jesus went in and out among us, 22 beginning from the baptism of John to that day when He was taken up from us, one of these must become a witness with us of His resurrection." 23 And they proposed two: Joseph called Barsabas, who was surnamed Justus, and Matthias. 24 And they prayed and said, "You, O Lord, who know the hearts of all, show which of these two You have chosen 25 to take part in this ministry and apostleship from which Judas by transgression fell, that he might go to his own place." 26 And they cast their lots, and the lot fell on Matthias. And he was numbered with the eleven apostles. —Acts 1:15–26

This event took place after these disciples had been praying a few days. We must remember the Holy Spirit had not yet been given, so their praying had to have been in their native tongues. Without the presence and the power of the Holy Spirit, Peter took it upon himself to act as spokesman and to declare to the group they needed to choose a replacement for Judas. Now his appraisal of the situation was accurate, a replacement did need to be chosen. But neither the Lord nor the Scriptures ever indicated it was the eleven disciples who were to do the choosing. The choice should have been left to the Lord.

"Yes, but didn't they pray and leave it to God to indicate which of the two men He had chosen?"

Yes. But there is no indication they prayed before they nominated these two men. They gave the Lord a choice, but how could they be sure they had nominated the man of His choice to begin with? Peter had pointed out what he considered to be the ideal qualifications for the replacement apostle, but the Bible never laid down those particular qualifications. Those were the qualifications for an apostle to Israel. However, there is a difference between an apostle to Israel and an apostle of the church of Jesus Christ. The apostle to Israel was sent only to the lost sheep of Israel. All of the eleven disciples fulfilled those qualifications, as did Justus and Matthias, but the day of Pentecost had not yet come. The Holy Spirit had not yet been poured out. The church age had not yet been ushered in. When that happened, the ministry gifts of apostle would be totally altered. No longer would a person be required to have been present from the ministry of John the Baptist until the time of the ascension in order to be an apostle.

Peter's assertion that the new apostle would have to be someone who was an eyewitness to the resurrection is not entirely valid either. What he didn't foresee was that a man named Saul of Tarsus could be a witness to that event on the road to Damascus when the resurrected Lord appeared to him personally.

The name Matthias is never mentioned again in any book of the New Testament. Historians never tell us what happened to him. Do you know why? God didn't choose Matthias. The disciples chose Matthias.

Now I didn't say there was never a twelfth apostle. There was. His name was Paul, "an apostle, [chosen] (not of men, neither by man, but [chosen] by Jesus Christ, and God the Father, who raised him from the dead)" (Galatians 1:1). What proof do we have that Paul was chosen by God as an apostle? In Acts 9:15, the Lord says to Ananias about Paul, "Go thy way: for he is a chosen vessel unto me, to bear my name before the Gentiles, and kings, and the children of Israel." Apostleship is not conferred by man or by men; it is conferred only by God.

G. Conferred upon Others Besides the Original Twelve Disciples

The seventh and final point we need to understand about apostleship is it can be conferred upon whomever the Lord desires. There are several instances in the New Testament in which it is evident people other than the twelve were recognized as apostles. Luke, the physician, numbers Barnabas among the apostles: "Which when the apostles, Barnabas and Paul, heard of, they rent their clothes, and ran in among the people, crying out" (Acts 14:14). Paul himself mentions at least four others whom he identifies as apostles:

1. James

18Then after three years I went up to Jerusalem to see Peter, and remained with him fifteen days. 19 But I saw none of the other apostles except James, the Lord's brother. —Galatians 1:18–19

After that, he was seen of James; then by all the apostles.
—1 Corinthians 15:7

2. Apollos

6 Now these things, brethren, I have figuratively transferred to myself and Apollos for your sakes, that you may learn in us not to think beyond what is written, that none of you may be puffed up on behalf of one against the other. 7 For who makes you differ from another? And what do you have that you did not receive? Now if you did indeed receive it, why do you boast as if you had not received it? 8 You are already full! You are already rich! You have reigned as kings without us—and indeed I could wish you did reign, that we also might reign with you! 9 For I think that God has displayed us, the apostles, last, as men condemned to death; for we have been made a spectacle to the world, both to angels and to men. —1 Corinthians 4:6–9

3. Silas and Timothy

Paul, Silvanus (Greek, Silas), and Timothy, To the church of the Thessalonians in God the Father and the Lord Jesus Christ: Grace to you and peace from God our Father and the Lord Jesus Christ. —1 Thessalonians 1:1

Nor did we seek glory from men, either from you or from others, when we might have made demands as apostles of Christ. —1 Thessalonians 2:6

I have stressed these seven points about apostleship because the book of Galatians is the strongest defense Paul makes of his ministry office. Nowhere else in his writings does he make a stronger declaration of his apostleship than in this book of Galatians. Throughout the book, he continually points out that from his mother's womb he had been chosen and set aside for the work God had for him to do. It was as though he wanted to make sure all credit for his ministry gifts would go to God the Father and the Lord Jesus Christ, not to man or to men.

1:2–14 God the Source

I. Grace Versus Legalism

Most books of the New Testament have one central theme. For example, the book of Ephesians deals with the church, and the book of Philippians has to do with joy. The theme of Galatians is grace versus legalism. It is a twofold theme: salvation by grace and spirituality by grace. Now when I use the term *legalism,* I am referring to the idea that something must be added to the grace of God either to obtain salvation or to attain spirituality. This usually implies some kind of works.

The basic theme of this letter deals with their mistaken idea that salvation and spirituality are not dependent solely upon the grace of God, but some other ingredient must be added to grace either to receive it or to remain in it.

To many, this idea seems ridiculous. We pride ourselves in thinking we would never be so foolish as to think we could ever do anything to merit God's favor. Yet there is a great lesson found in this book, because we often come much closer to this way of thinking than we realize.

We know salvation is by faith plus nothing. We quote Ephesians 2:89, "For by grace are ye saved through faith; and that not of yourselves: it is the gift of God: not of works, lest any man should boast."

We know full well salvation is not obtained through any self-effort; it is received as a free gift from God through faith in His Son Jesus Christ. We read it is "not by works of righteousness which we have done, but according to his mercy he saved us" (Titus 3:5). We readily accept the biblical truth that all our self-righteousness is as filthy rags in the sight of God (Isaiah 64:6), and it is only by the washing of regeneration and renewing of the Holy Spirit that we are made clean. All this and more we believe and confess.

Yet even knowing we have been saved by grace through faith, we would never think for a moment we might lose our salvation. We know better than that. Deep down inside we still harbor a fear that we will somehow not be pleasing to God; we will "fall short of the glory" (Romans 3:23 NIV) and not measure up to "the stature of the fulness of Christ" (Ephesians 4:13).

In other words, although we know we are saved by grace, we can't help feeling to some extent that we have to work out our salvation (with the emphasis on *work)*. Despite all our claims to total dependence upon the grace of God, we still feel obligated to do something. It's difficult for us to believe we don't have to be careful to keep all the dos and don'ts if we're going to be truly spiritual.

As understandable as this attitude may be, it is still legalism, just like believing that circumcision or observance of some other part of the Jewish law is necessary for salvation or spirituality. We tend to be legalistic in our thinking, even if that legalism just involves doing good works, attending church services faithfully, paying tithes, teaching a Sunday school class, praising God, praying, or even reading our Bible. We should do these things because we love the Lord, not to gain His attention and approval.

Legalism takes our eyes off of God and others and centers them on ourselves. We become so concerned with *our* thoughts, *our* words, and *our* actions that we lose sight of the Lord and of others. We begin to do what we do out of a sense of obligation rather than out of a heart of love and concern. Even witnessing can become legalistic if we witness because we feel obligated to instead of being motivated by our love for people.

There is also the whole range of rules and regulations we hear in many churches that place great emphasis upon holiness. Dress length, sleeve length, whether or not it is proper to wear jewelry or makeup, whether a Christian should own a television set or go to the movies or swim in mixed company (or swim at all) and on and on. Churches that focus on laws soon lose their zeal for evangelism. They become so engrossed in themselves and their rules and codes, they cut themselves off from the very people they need to be meeting and witnessing to and winning. As a result, they eventually dry up from within.

Getting our eyes off of God and others and onto ourselves is exactly what the devil wants us to do. Once we start looking either at our own self-righteousness or at our own shortcomings and failures, he has us trapped because we will no longer reach out to bless and win others.

Paul knew all this. That's why he wrote this strongly worded letter to the churches in Galatia. He was vitally concerned because they were falling victim to legalism because he knew, as he told the Corinthians, the letter of the law "killeth, but the spirit giveth life" (2 Corinthians 3:6).

In order to fully understand and appreciate Paul's message to the Galatians, we need to back up a bit and lay the foundation of what had transpired before this letter was penned. Paul was not an apostle to the Jews. He was an apostle to the Gentiles. On his first missionary tour, he and Barnabas went to the area of Galatia where they saw many people born again, filled with the Spirit, healed, and blessed. They organized these people into churches, got them started on their Christian walk, and then left to minister in other areas.

However, as soon as Paul and Barnabas had departed, zealous Jews (those who had a hard time breaking away from the law) came to investigate Paul's ministry. And when they discovered the message Paul had preached was grace — salvation through simple faith in Jesus Christ — they immediately began to teach these Gentile converts about the Jewish law.

These converts had never heard about the law. Paul hadn't taught them they were freed from the law because they had never been under the law. Naturally, as soon as the Jewish leaders came in and began to teach them about the law, they began to try to observe it. They started trying to combine the law and grace.

Suddenly confusion reigned. These people were trying to live in grace yet keep every jot and tittle of the Jewish law, which they knew nothing about. Paul had to write them to explain they were under no obligation to live by a set of rules and regulations Jesus Christ fulfilled for them at the cross.

With this background in mind, let's continue our study of Galatians.

II. Authority Established (2)

1:2 and all the brethren who are with me, ¶ To the churches of Galatia:

Paul continues to emphasize his qualifications and authority as an apostle of Jesus Christ by pointing out he is not alone in this ministry, but is accompanied by other well-qualified and recognized leaders in the church. He is well aware of what has happened in Galatia in his absence, how the legalistic Judaizers had come in to refute Christ's message of grace and to cast doubt on his character and apostleship. That was the reason he begins this letter in verse 1 with the bold assertion that his ordination and authority as an apostle came directly from God and not from any man or group of men.

Here in verse 2, he is quick to point out that although he is personally chosen (hand-picked by the Lord Himself) he does not stand alone — he operates with a team. There is a lesson here for us today. We have each been chosen and elected by God to minister in His name. Yet we too must realize none of us stand alone. Like individual members of a team, we must all work together in harmony and unified purpose if we are to accomplish what God has called us to do. As members of the body of Christ, none of us must think of ourselves as some great high and mighty person to whom others owe allegiance and servitude. Even our Lord said He came not to be ministered to, but to minister and give His life a ransom for many. He also made it abundantly clear that he who would be greatest in the kingdom of God must be servant to all (Mark 10:42–45).

Even though we have been individually chosen and anointed by God, we are nothing special in ourselves. We must remember all believers have also been individually chosen and anointed for the work the Lord has set them apart to do. If any of us are to succeed in our assigned tasks, it will require joint effort, teamwork. We are all individual members of a super-natural team under the leadership of the Holy Spirit of God. Each must contribute to the overall goal of that team by fulfilling his own individual assignment and by assisting the other team members to fulfill theirs. God works with us as a team, not as "stars."

Even the great apostle Paul worked as a member of a team. The rest of the team was made up of Titus, Silas, Luke, Timothy, Tychicus, and Trophimus. At the time of this writing, the other team members were not physically present with Paul. They were spread throughout the province of Asia, but they were one with him in purpose and goal. They were the ones to whom Paul was referring when he sent greetings to the churches in Galatia from those who were with him in the ministry.

III. Grace and Peace (3)

1:3 ⸿ Grace to you and peace from God the Father and our Lord Jesus Christ,

Paul gets right into the theme of this book: the grace of God. He points out from the beginning that grace comes from "God the Father, and from our Lord Jesus Christ." These people in Galatia had left grace and had gone into works. That is the basic problem Paul is addressing, even in his greeting.

If grace comes from God, then where do works come from? From man. "Grace be to you and peace from God," not from men. Men don't give grace and peace; they prescribe works. They set up religions. Someone said that Christianity is what God has done for man in Christ, while religion is what man tries to do for God in his own strength. Religion is not founded on God's grace, the gift of God's unmerited favor, but on works, man's attempt to gain God's favor by his own efforts. This is why Paul is so hard on those who are foolish enough to turn from grace to works.

"Grace be to you and peace." Peace is the product of grace. If you will notice carefully, you will see whenever you leave the true message of God's grace and start trying to mix anything else with it, the first thing you will begin to lose is peace. You will become frustrated. If you are trying to build your Christian life on human works, sooner or later you will experience frustration.

There is a simple principle involved here. You simply cannot please God by works. There is only one thing that pleases God. We find it spelled out for us in Hebrews 11:6: "But without faith it is impossible to please him." It's not difficult to please God by works; it's impossible. Nothing pleases God but faith in the finished work of Jesus Christ on the cross. Anything we add to that finished work displeases our heavenly Father and results in our loss of peace.

Am I saying then that works are wrong? No, not at all. Works are fine. We are supposed to work, just as our Lord worked: "But I have greater witness than that of John: for the works which the Father hath given me to finish, the same works that I do, bear witness of me, that the Father hath sent me" (John 5:36). Later in John 14:10, Jesus explained how those works were done: "Believest thou not that I am in the Father, and the Father in me? the words that I speak unto you I speak not of myself: but the Father that dwelleth in me, he doeth the works."

We remember our Lord told us he who believed in Him would do the same works He did and even greater works (John 14:12). But how? He gave us that answer in John 15:5: "I am the vine, ye are the branches: He that abideth in me, and I in him, the same bringeth forth much fruit: for without me ye can do nothing." Fruit (good works) is produced through us not because of anything we are or do of ourselves, but because of the Word that abides in us. Works are produced by the same indwelling Spirit who did the works through Jesus. Works are evidence of God's favor upon us, not a means to obtain or retain His favor. We remain in God's favor by remaining in fellowship with Him and His Word, not by works of might.

So we do work, but not to please God. We work because He has blessed us so much in grace we just want to work for Him. It's not the works we do that please God; it's the faith we exercise in Him. It's not giving itself that pleases God; it's the faith we demonstrate when we freely give out of hearts of thanksgiving and praise for all His blessings upon us. We don't give as an act of obedience or obligation or duty. We don't "owe" God His ten percent. What does He need with our measly ten percent when the whole universe belongs to Him? He managed just fine without our tithe before we came along, and He will continue to do just fine without it after we're gone.

It's not the ten percent that pleases God; it's the freedom and unselfishness we display by our giving. God doesn't look at the amount of the gift; He looks at the attitude of the giver. The Bible doesn't say the Lord loves a big giver, it says He loves a "cheerful giver" (2 Corinthians 9:7).

Then there is witnessing. Some church people make witnessing such a burden and a task they destroy the whole purpose and meaning behind it. Either they make it out to be a quota that every Christian must fill, thus producing all kinds of guilt in those who don't feel they have met the standard, or they make it out to be some kind of contest in which the one who gets the most converts wins the prize of God's favor and blessing. I have never understood any concept of witnessing that sees it as a means of "buttering up" God or winning "brownie points." Witnessing is not meant to be a chore or a contest. It is supposed to be the natural consequence of a heart so filled with joy and peace in the Lord, it cannot help but speak of the one who is the source of that blessing.

Like works, witnessing is not wrong, but many times our concept of it is wrong. Witnessing is good if we witness for the right reason.

T. L. Osborn loved to tell about the old Methodist preacher who used to ask his parishioners, "Has the Lord done anything so good for you that you just can't keep quiet about it?" When God so freely provides for you that you just want to do something for Him, that's witnessing! You want to work for Him. You want to clean the church carpet, sweep the floor, take up the offering, serve Communion, work in the nursery, teach a Sunday school class, visit the sick — tell others about Him. Not to get a gold star by your name on God's "bless-me" list, but simply because you want to bless others as you have been blessed. That's grace!

Once you understand grace, you begin to understand peace. When you can receive God's grace, then you are in a position to receive His peace.

When I was a youth, I was in a church camp with a girl who had been raised on the dos and don'ts. All her life she had tried to live by a strict religious code. At camp that year the leader taught on the theme of our being complete in Christ. He kept hammering away at the fact that if a person is complete, he can't get any "completer." The more he talked on that subject and the more the girl listened, the more she became aware of the truth of that message. For the first time in her life, she began to realize she didn't have to work for holiness (wholeness); she was already complete (whole) in her Savior. Finally she broke down in tears, weeping with joy and relief.

"I see it; it's all God's grace," she sobbed. "I feel as if a ten-ton weight has been lifted off my back. I don't have to try to please God anymore; He is already pleased with me. That puts a whole different light on it. Now I want to work for Him rather than have to work for Him."

The moment she understood grace, peace overwhelmed her. Oh, if only more Christians could come to that understanding. The faith life is not trying to please God by our action, even our great faith. It's just living by the principles of the Word He has already provided. Salvation, peace, prosperity, success, health, joy, life in all its fullness and abundance, has already been provided for us by our loving heavenly Father. If that's so, then we don't need to try to obtain His blessings by winning His favor. We already have His favor, His grace. It was His grace that moved Him to do all this for us in the first place. We simply need to receive the blessings that accompany His favor.

IV. Deliverance (4)

1:4 who gave Himself for our sins, that He might deliver us from this present evil age, according to the will of our God and Father,

Who gave himself for our sins, . . .

The Greek word translated "for" actually means in exchange for. Jesus Christ gave Himself in exchange for our sins.

You see, throughout the Word of God, we read that Jesus took the curse of the law upon Himself and gave us the blessing of God in its place. We received redemption, but what did He receive? Sin. We received righteousness. What did He receive? Unrighteousness. We received riches. He took poverty. We have healing. He became sickness. Don't you like that trade? Isn't it wonderful to know Jesus took all our sin, unrighteousness, poverty, and sickness upon Himself and in return gave us His holiness, righteousness, riches, and health? That's what happened at the cross of Calvary. That is the truth Paul wants these Galatians to understand right from the outset. Jesus gave Himself in exchange.

. . . That he might deliver us from this present evil world, . . .

The word translated "world" is actually from the Greek word for age. The world itself is not evil; it's the age in which we live that is evil. The world, God's creation, is good; it has just been corrupted by the evil that is loose in it. It is this present evil age. That means it will not last forever; it is only temporary. Jesus is coming soon. It's also comforting to know in the midst of this present age of sin, sickness, poverty, and misery you and I can live in righteousness, health, riches, happiness, and joy. All this is because of the exchange that took place at Calvary.

Notice also this word "deliver." Deliverance is potential, that "he might deliver us." If there are people in this evil age who are not delivered from it, it is not God's fault, it's their fault. Salvation, and all that goes with it, is potential. Jesus Christ has done everything He could do to remove sin and unrighteousness from people. He took it all upon Himself when He was nailed to the cross. In exchange, He gave us His righteousness, prosperity, and peace. He traded His salvation for our sin, but He will not force that exchange upon anyone. It must be accepted by each person individually. Unless a person does that for himself, he cannot benefit from the exchange.

. . . According to the will of God and our Father; . . .

In the original Greek, the word "and" does not appear. This phrase should read, "According to the will of God our Father." What is the will of our Father? The apostle Peter said God is "not willing that any should perish, but that all should come to repentance" (2 Peter 3:9). And from John we learn God's commandment is "that we should believe on the name of his Son Jesus Christ" (1 John 3:23). Jesus said He was sent to this earth by the Father so those who believe in Him might have life, "and that they might have it more abundantly" (John 10:10). It is obvious it is God's will for everyone to be born again and enjoy eternal and abundant life.

Eternal life does not begin when we die; it begins when we receive the Lord Jesus Christ. In the same way, abundant life is not something just laid up for us in heaven; it also begins here and now. Grace doesn't end at salvation; it continues every day of our lives, now and forever.

We read these words written by David in Psalms 103:

> 2 Bless the Lord, O my soul, And forget not all His benefits 3
> Who forgives all your iniquities, Who heals all your diseases, 4
> Who redeems your life from destruction, Who crowns you with

lovingkindness and tender mercies, 5 Who satisfies your mouth
with good things, So that your youth is renewed like the eagle's.
—Psalm 103:2–5

If you are not enjoying all God's blessings of forgiveness, healing, redemption, loving-kindness, mercy, prosperity, and strength, then perhaps it is
because you have simply forgotten all His benefits. In Jesus Christ, God
has already done all He can do to bless you. The next move is up to you.

I picture the plan of salvation (deliverance) like a game of checkers. God
has made His move; now it's our turn. He has done His part; now He's
waiting for us to do ours. Our part is simply to receive what He did for us
at Calvary.

Some people say faith moves God. That's not true. Faith doesn't move
God; God has already moved. Faith moves us into a position to receive
what God has already done. The Bible is one long recitation of God's
movement throughout history, culminating in the cross where the great
exchange took place. There God took our sins, laid them on His own Son,
and then nailed them to the cross, freeing us from them forever. In their
place He gave us His righteousness. That exchange is complete. God has
done His part. Now it's our move; that move is to accept what He has already done in Jesus Christ.

No one who goes to hell can ever blame the Lord for his condemnation.
God made the first move. If the person refuses to accept what was done
for him in Christ, that's his fault, not God's.

The same can be said of the born-again believer who goes through life
beaten down and defeated because he has not received the fullness of
God's grace and love. If that is your situation, it's your fault, not God's. He
has done His part. You now need to do yours. You receive the abundant
life in the same way you received eternal life, by simple faith. Believe on
the Lord Jesus Christ, and you will be saved (healed, prospered, restored,
set free, delivered).

V. To Whom Be Glory (5)

1:5 to whom *be* glory forever and ever. Amen.

Notice the last word in this fifth verse, "Amen." Now we are accustomed
to this word coming at the conclusion of a prayer or hymn or sermon. To
us it marks the end of an utterance or thought, but here we find it inserted

between the fifth and sixth verses of the very first chapter of this book. Why?

The reason is obvious. This word marks the conclusion of Paul's greeting or opening remarks. In three verses (vv. 3–5), Paul gave the entire plan of salvation, ending it with an "amen." For all practical purposes, he could have ended the letter right there. He has actually said everything he needs to say. It is regrettable that from verse 6 to the end of the book he has to talk about the problems in the Galatian churches. The solution is given in three verses, but the discussion of the problem takes an additional five and three quarter chapters.

This brief opening section contains the whole plan of salvation. But is there anything mentioned in it about the Jewish law? Any discussion of animal sacrifice? What about circumcision? Nothing said about dietary restrictions? No dress code? No lists of dos and don'ts? No "do this and live"?

None. The whole plan of salvation is summarized in one concept: Jesus Christ went to the cross for our sins, so we might be delivered from this present evil age. Amen.

VI. Another Gospel (6–9)

In these verses Paul nails down the problem. In most of his books, Paul starts out with a message of tremendous edification. In Ephesians, for example, he began by telling the believers in Ephesus about all God did for them in times past, how He had blessed them with all spiritual blessings, how they had been redeemed, and how wonderful the things of God were. But in Galatians, Paul launches right into the problem at hand. He immediately levels a scathing accusation against these people for being so foolish as to fall for "different gospel."

> **1:6 ⸆ I marvel that you are turning away so soon from Him who called you in the grace of Christ, to a different gospel,**

This expression "I marvel" could be translated I am astonished or I am shocked. "So soon" refers to the few months in which Paul has been absent from these people.

I marvel that ye are so soon removed from him that called you into the grace of Christ unto another gospel:

The word translated "removed" is actually a Greek military term meaning to go AWOL (absent without leave). Paul was saying, "I am shocked to hear that some of you who joined ranks with the Lord Jesus Christ have so quickly deserted!"

I'm sure those who read this letter said to themselves, "We haven't deserted!" But they had. To turn away from the grace of God by mixing anything with it is to go AWOL. It is to climb over the fence and run away.

Notice in this verse Paul again refers to the grace of Christ. In verse 3, he prays grace and peace would be theirs. Now here in verses 6 and 7, he tells them they have removed themselves from the grace of Christ to follow "another gospel: which is not another." That may seem a little confusing, so let's look at this term "another gospel."

How could these people be following "another gospel: which is not another"? In the Greek there are two words for "another." One is *heteros* and the other is *allos. Heteros* means another of a different kind. *Allos* means another of the same kind. In the *King James Version,* both are translated by the same English word "another," but they do not have exactly the same meaning. For example, if someone gave you an apple and then handed you an orange, they would both be pieces of fruit, but the second one would be *heteros*, another of a different kind. If, however, you had one apple and someone gave you a second apple, it would be *allos*, another of the same kind.

Paul is saying, "I am shocked that you have so soon deserted Him who called you into the grace of Christ to follow after another gospel of a different kind, which is not another of the same kind." In other words, Paul reveals to these people that the Jews are telling them their legalistic message was just another form of the gospel, but it wasn't. It was "another gospel," but it was most definitely not the true gospel of the Lord Jesus Christ. It was *heteros*, another gospel of a different kind than what Paul and Barnabas had preached in Galatia.

Is there such a thing as an *allos*, another gospel of the same kind? Yes, there is. The Bible mentions the gospel of grace, the gospel of the kingdom, the gospel of peace, and more. All these are gospels of the same kind. They all refer to the same gospel; they just emphasize different aspects of it. When something other than grace is mixed in with that gospel message, it ceases to be a different form of the same gospel and becomes a different "gospel" altogether. That's what Paul is telling these people about the new Jewish "gospel" they had been so quick to embrace.

1:7 which is not another; but there are some who trouble you and want to pervert the gospel of Christ.

Perverting the gospel of Christ refers to mixing something in with it. The Bible pronounces a curse on anyone who dares to add to or take away from the gospel (Revelation 22:18–19). To do so is to pervert it into another gospel of a different kind. Later on in Galatians Paul points out that a little leaven leavens the whole loaf. Leaven refers to some foreign object added to dough to make it rise. It makes it appear bigger than it really is because it is puffed up. That's what foreign matter does to the gospel; it puffs it up to make it appear to be something it is not.

Leaven also speeds up the manifestation. Many times people will try to speed up the manifestation of whatever they are praying and exercising faith to receive. For instance, they may be believing for an extra $500 for a need. It is always a temptation to help God out a little by letting rich Aunt Suzie know about the prayer request. Such an attempt to take matters into their own hands while supposedly trusting God is a good example of adding a little leaven to the lump. Even though people may try to justify their lack of faith by asking what harm it would do to just speed things along a bit, the answer is obvious. Either they are depending solely on God or they are not. There is no middle ground. To try to hedge faith is to deny it altogether.

"Yes, but sometimes it's quicker to sort of take things into your own hands than to wait on God to move. Sometimes the faith way just takes so long!"

Yes, it does, but while you are waiting and exercising patience, your faith is being perfected. The next time you step out in faith, it won't take quite so long. You will have grown, matured. What you receive from God by faith is always like a seed; it has the capacity of increasing again and again, but not if you bail out before God's manifestation arrives. Such an action indicates a lack of patience to see faith through to its completion. You have perverted the gospel by mixing self-effort with it. That's what Paul was berating the Galatians for.

1:8–9 But even if we, or an angel from heaven, preach any other gospel to you than what we have preached to you, let him be accursed. 9 As we have said before, so now I say again, if anyone preaches any other gospel to you than what you have received, let him be accursed.

. . .We. . . an angel . . .anyone. . . .

These three terms cover just about any way a person could hear the Word of God. Paul is making it clear. If anyone, whoever he might be, preaches a gospel other than the true gospel of Jesus Christ, that person is accursed, and if any person preaches the true gospel, he is blessed.

This is an important point. Paul is stressing it's not the messenger who matters; it's the message that is important. So often we get our eyes on the messenger and take them off the message. We become so enamored with the great preachers, we don't hear what those closest to us have to say.

Why didn't we believe it when we heard it the first time? We didn't believe it because we put more emphasis on the messenger who delivered it than on the message itself. That is dangerous. God speaks to us in many ways and through many people, many times through those we least esteem. We need to recognize the message of the Lord as surely as we recognize the Lord Himself.

VII. Not to Please Man (10)

1:10 ¶ For do I now persuade men, or God? Or do I seek to please men? For if I still pleased men, I would not be a bond-servant of Christ.

For do I now persuade men . . .

By this expression Paul meant, "Am I trying to appeal to men?" If that were the case, then Paul would be going along with what these Jews were saying to the Galatians. Instead, he was standing firm against them and their gospel. It seemed Paul was standing alone, but there was a team with him, though at times it seemed even they were against him. Oftentimes that's the way it is in the ministry. When you embark on the faith walk, you will soon discover not everybody is going to rally around you to support you in your every decision and stance. In fact, you will soon find where your faith really lies, in men or in God.

. . .For if I yet pleased men, I should not be the servant of Christ.

Notice this word "yet." Paul used this word because at one time in his life all he sought was to please men. When he was Saul of Tarsus, the zealous Pharisee, his whole existence was wrapped up in pleasing the powers that be, so much so he hunted and persecuted the church so he could advance himself in the Jewish religion.

But no more. Now his whole life is devoted to pleasing God, even if it means being persecuted himself, as he `was, repeatedly, until the end of his days. That's the price of apostleship. Paul knew what so many of us have learned: In order to be a servant of Christ, a person has to be prepared to suffer the opposition of man. A servant pleases his master. If you seek to please men, they are your masters; you are a servant to men. Be a servant of Christ, and please Him.

VIII. Religion Versus the Gospel

Notice the contrast Paul makes between the gospel of Jesus Christ and the religion of the Jews to which he himself was at one time totally dedicated.

> **1:11–12 ¶ But I make known to you, brethren, that the gospel which was preached by me is not according to man. 12 For I neither received it from man, nor was I taught *it*, but *it came* through the revelation of Jesus Christ.**

The first difference is religion comes from the minds of men and is passed on through their teachings, but the gospel comes directly from Jesus Christ through personal revelation. Here again Paul was stressing that his apostleship came from the Lord and not from man or men.

> **1:13 ¶ For you have heard of my former conduct in Judaism, how I persecuted the church of God beyond measure and *tried* to destroy it.**

For ye have heard of my conversation in time past in the Jews' religion, how that beyond measure I persecuted the church of God, and wasted it:

Here Paul begins to get into his former life. The word "conversation" here implies a way of life. "Time past" refers to that time before his conversion. Paul is describing his lifestyle before he met Jesus Christ face-to-face on the Damascus road.

Note carefully the next expression: "the Jews' religion." Judaism is a religion and religion is man's effort to achieve salvation through his own efforts. That's why Paul goes on to stress how zealous he was when he was religious. In Philippians 3:4 through 6, he described how devout he was, referring to himself as "a Hebrew of the Hebrews" (v. 5), and claiming that in matters of the Jewish law he was "blameless" (v. 6). Yet he wrote to Timothy, "This is a faithful saying, and worthy of all acceptation, that Christ Jesus came into the world to save sinners; of whom I am chief" (1 Timothy 1:15). Paul had learned by personal experience that "by the works of the law shall no flesh be justified" (Galatians 2:16).

If personal works could save anyone, Saul of Tarsus would have been a shining example of salvation. If self-effort could save even one person, Jesus would not have had to die on the cross. Saul not only came face-to-face with Jesus on the road to Damascus, he also came face-to-face with himself, the chief of sinners.

1:14 And I advanced in Judaism beyond many of my contemporaries in my own nation, being more exceedingly zealous for the traditions of my fathers.

Notice that word "traditions." That is a good definition of religion. Paul knows firsthand about religion. That's why he is so aware of the dangers of trusting in the traditions of men rather than in the grace of God. He knows religion is probably the worst thing that has ever happened since the fall of man. Of all the sins and evils we can think of, religion is by far the worst. Religion has caused more people to miss salvation than all the other sins and evil combined. Not only that, religion has been the worst persecutor of the church in the history of mankind.

No dictator, tyrant, or totalitarian regime has ever come anywhere close to causing as much damage to the church of Jesus Christ that religion has. The sad part is all the persecution, misery, and suffering religion has caused has been done in the name of God!

Look at many Hindu nations today, filled with disease, famine, dissension, and hatred, where thousands of people are literally starving to death in the streets while food walks right past them. Yet they will not kill and eat the food available because according to their religion, cattle is sacred. They are taught that a cow might be the reincarnated form of their own relative! That's what religion does to people. It blinds them to the truth while it destroys them physically, mentally, and spiritually.

Religion blinds people to the gospel. Of all the people I have ever witnessed to about the Lord Jesus Christ, religious people are by far the most difficult to win. They are so proud of their traditions, rituals, and good deeds that it is almost impossible for them to receive salvation by simple faith. Consider the rich young ruler who came to Jesus seeking salvation. He was so devoted to his strict observance of the law he could not let go of either his earthly possessions or his own self-righteousness. Religion, with its emphasis on self-examination and self-achievement, has robbed more sinners of their salvation (and more Christians of their joy and peace) than any evil under the sun. It is hard for people to receive when they are convinced they must achieve.

Paul is a prime example. When Paul stated he had "profited" in the Jewish religion, he meant he had advanced in it. He did that by persecuting the church of Jesus Christ. The more he advanced, the more determined he became to destroy every Christian he could find. The more Christians he destroyed, the faster he advanced. He was caught in a vicious cycle. Sooner or later something had to give. It was either the church or Saul of Tarsus.

When Jesus said the gates of hell would not prevail against His church (Matt. 16:18), He meant exactly what He said. Therefore, it was not the church that fell; it was Saul — on the road to Damascus. He fell to the ground at the feet of a risen Savior and arose a new creature. From that day, Saul of Tarsus became Paul, "an apostle, (not of men, neither by man, but by Jesus Christ, and God the Father)" (Galatians 1:1). Remember the meaning of the word apostle? Paul was instantly promoted from "chief of sinners" to "a sent one" in the church of Jesus Christ. That's the difference between what religion does to us and what the gospel does for us.

1:15–2:10 Paul's Revelation

I. Revelation Precedes Proclamation (15–16)

1:15 ¶ But when it pleased God, who separated me from my mother's womb and called *me* through His grace,

But when it pleased God, who separated me from my mother's womb . . .

Paul said he was "separated" (set aside for service to God) before he was born. This can also be said of you and me, of every true believer in Jesus Christ. In Ephesians 1:3 and 4, Paul wrote to the believers in Ephesus, "Blessed be the God and Father of our Lord Jesus Christ, who hath blessed us with all spiritual blessings in heavenly places in Christ: according as he hath chosen us in him before the foundation of the world, that we should be holy and without blame before him in love."

. . . and called me by his grace,

If God chose Paul before he was born, that must be grace, because how could Paul work for something bestowed upon him in his mother's womb? This choosing of Paul was not an isolated incident, as we have seen in Ephesians 1. Rather, each child of God is chosen before the foundation of the world. It is not only Paul who is saved and sanctified by grace, but every believer, before we ever have opportunity to work for, earn, or deserve it. Salvation is not dependent upon anything a person does; it rests solely upon the grace of God.

Everything in the Christian life is grace. Like Paul, you and I were chosen before the foundation of the world to fulfill the particular ministries to which the Lord has called us. Many Christians think they have no ministry because they are not involved in full-time church work. But the truth is, in the New Testament church there is no distinction made between the clergy and the laity. Every member of the body of Christ is in full-time Christian service, whether he knows it or not, whether he fulfills it or not.

If you are a Christian, you are a minister of the gospel of Jesus Christ. Like Paul, you are separated and called by God's grace to preach the gospel to those to whom He will lead you, those whom no one else but you can reach.

1:16 to reveal His Son in me, that I might preach Him among the Gentiles, I did not immediately confer with flesh and blood,

Notice what Paul said about the purpose of God's revelation of His Son to him: "that I might preach." There is a sequence here. Revelation always precedes proclamation. No one can truly preach who has not first received revelation from God.

In my ministry I meet so many young people who seem to have the idea that since the return of the Lord Jesus to this earth is so imminent, they don't have time to fully prepare themselves for ministry. They are so afraid time will run out before they get on the field, they rush into ministry without adequate training and instruction.

"Oh, I'd love to be able to go to Bible school or get my seminary degree, but there's no time. I've got to get started preaching right away!"

"No, you don't," I tell them. "You don't have anything to preach yet."

"Oh, but I've been called."

"I'm sure you have. But there is a sequence to be followed here. First comes the call, then the revelation, then the preaching. We are all called to preach the gospel, but that doesn't mean we're ready to start preaching as soon as we are born again. Like every other one of God's blessings, ministry requires time and preparation."

"Oh, but what if Jesus comes back while I'm still in school?"

"Well, if He does, so be it. Personally, if Jesus came, I'd rather be in school preparing to preach than out there preaching with nothing to say."

If you are called to the ministry, get yourself in a place where God can teach you, where you can be instructed and prepared mentally and emotionally as well as spiritually. That's what Paul did.

To reveal his Son in me, that I might preach him among the heathen; . . .

Notice, not only did Paul receive a definite call to the apostleship, as a "sent one," he knew he was sent to "the heathen." This word appears many times in the book of Galatians. So does the word *Gentiles*. These two words are the same word in Greek. It is the word *ethne*, from which we derive our English word *ethnic*, having to do with race or native origin. In this verse the word refers to the non-Jews. Peter was primarily called to minister the gospel to the Hebrews and Paul was set aside as an apostle to the Gentiles. Later on these two groups will also be referred to as the circumcision and the uncircumcision (cf. Galatians 2:7, Colossians 3:11).

. . . Immediately I conferred not with flesh and blood,

This is very important. After Paul received his call, his ordination as an apostle, not of men, neither by man, but by God the Father and the Lord Jesus Christ, he noted he did not confer with a man, with flesh and blood. Paul understands that revelation knowledge does not come from flesh and blood, but is always of divine origin.

Do you remember what Jesus told Peter when he identified Him as the Christ, the Son of the Living God? "Blessed art thou, Simon Barjona: for flesh and blood hath not revealed it unto thee, but my Father which is in heaven" (Matthew 16:17). Paul received his call to the ministry directly from God and was told to preach to the Gentiles, just as the Lord had told Ananias He was setting him aside to do (Acts 9:15).

II. Into the Wilderness (17)

1:17 nor did I go up to Jerusalem to those *who were* apostles before me; but I went to Arabia, and returned again to Damascus.

At this time Jerusalem was the center of religious activity of the day. It was the headquarters of the Jewish religion as well as the focal point of the Christian church.

. . . To them which were apostles before me; . . .

Paul is saying, once he received God's call upon his life, he did not immediately consult with the leaders of the church. He did not confer with men. He felt no obligation or need to run to James, the pastor of the church in Jerusalem, to seek counsel of him. Instead he went to God.

Paul did finally meet with James and Peter, but there is no indication he felt inferior to them in any way or that he tried to use his personal revelation from God to lord it over them. That should be a lesson to us. We are not subservient to church officials any more than we are to any other man. At the same time, we are not to feel or act superior to anyone because we have received revelation knowledge from God. If we have such knowledge, people will come to recognize it and its source. Yet in this statement, Paul reveals he considers himself to be an apostle of equal rank with the others because he pointed out that he did not confer with those who were apostles "before him." I believe Paul is the twelfth apostle, the one chosen by the Lord Himself to take the place of Judas.

. . . But I went into Arabia, . . .

At the time this was written, the region called Arabia covered a huge area. How long Paul remained there we don't know. The interesting thing about this statement is that Arabia was Gentile territory. It was there Paul received the full revelation from God that he would later share in his writings. Paul was thus the second graduate of Arabia. Moses was the first.

Moses spent forty years tending sheep in Midian where he received his call from the Lord to lead the children of Israel out of Egypt and into the Promised Land. When Jesus was anointed with the Holy Spirit upon His baptism by John the Baptist in the Jordan River, He too was led of the Spirit of God into the wilderness. It would seem there is always a time of solitary reflection and preparation that accompanies the call to ministry.

"And returned again unto Damascus." The word "again" indicates Paul left from Damascus (after his conversion on the road) to go into Arabia, and then returned after his time alone with the Lord. We read about this event in the ninth chapter of Acts, which describes Paul's conversion on the road to Damascus, Ananias praying for his eyes to be opened and that he be filled with the Holy Spirit, and finally, his baptism in water. (See verses 1–18.) Acts 9:19–22 tell us:

> 19 So when he had received food, he was strengthened. Then Saul spent some days with the disciples at Damascus. 20 Immediately he preached the Christ in the synagogues, that He is the Son of God. 21 Then all who heard were amazed, and said, "Is this not he who destroyed those who called on this name in Jerusalem, and has come here for that purpose, so that he might bring them bound to the chief priests?" 22 But Saul increased all the more in strength, and confounded the Jews who dwelt in Damascus, proving that this Jesus is the Christ. —Acts 9:19–22

Immediately after his conversion Paul began to preach Jesus Christ was the Son of God, a basic salvation message. You can't preach what you don't have. At that time Paul only knew the Lord as his Savior based on his own personal experience. Those called into the preaching ministry should not go beyond what we know, beyond our own experience because a witness is one who testifies of what he himself has seen and heard. Paul didn't begin by holding great evangelistic crusades; he began by simply preaching what he knew — that Jesus Christ is the Son of God.

However, it wasn't long before his field of personal experience and knowledge began to grow. As his strength increased, so did his powers of persuasion and influence. So will ours, if we are faithful enough to preach only what we know and patient enough to keep on preaching it until we know more. As our knowledge increases, so will our ministry.

III. Paul in Jerusalem (18–20)

1:18–19 ¶ Then after three years I went up to Jerusalem to see Peter, and remained with him fifteen days. ¹⁹ But I saw none of the other apostles except James, the Lord's brother.

Verse 18 fits into the time frame between verses 22 and 23 of Acts 9:

²³ Now after many days were past, the Jews plotted to kill him. ²⁴ But their plot became known to Saul. And they watched the gates day and night, to kill him. ²⁵ Then the disciples took him by night and let *him* down through the wall in a large basket. —Acts 9: 23–25

This expression "many days" refers to the period of three years Paul mentioned in Galatians 1:18. It was during this time Paul made his journey into Arabia where he received his New Testament revelation from God. How long that revelation lasted we don't know for sure, but we do know from Paul's other writings this was time well spent. Afterward Paul returned to Damascus where he began to preach and teach in the Jewish synagogue. His message so stirred up the Jews he had to flee for his life.

When he got to Jerusalem, he spent two weeks with Peter. Wouldn't you love to have been present to hear Paul share with Peter all the Lord had revealed to him? I'm sure it was good for Peter, because no one needed a good stable foundation more than Simon. We know he benefited from his association with Paul because later on in his own epistles he made reference to Paul's writings, noting they were far advanced and contained many things hard to understand, but needful to the body of Christ (2 Peter 3:15–16).

1:20 (Now *concerning* the things which I write to you, indeed, before God, I do not lie.)

Paul said "I do not lie" because the legalistic Judaizers had come into Galatia behind him to stir up the people by casting doubt upon his message and his qualifications as an apostle. Paul had to defend his apostleship against these men whose purpose was to lead the uninformed and impressionable Galatians back into the bondage of the law.

If you go into the ministry of the Word, it is likely your greatest opposition will also be from established religion. Like Paul, you may find yourself the object of ridicule and scorn. If so, don't be surprised or overcome by it. Above all, don't give in to anger and retaliation. Be firm in your beliefs but operate in love both toward those who hear you gladly and those who oppose you and your message. Paul exercised his authority as an apostle, but he always did it in a spirit of love. So should we, for how can we ever convince the world (and the church) of God's love for them, if we don't demonstrate that love ourselves?

IV. The Proving Time (21–24)

> **1:21–23 ¶ Afterward I went into the regions of Syria and Cilicia. 22 And I was unknown by face to the churches of Judea which *were* in Christ. 23 But they were hearing only, "He who formerly persecuted us now preaches the faith which he once *tried to* destroy."**

After staying in Antioch for some time, Paul made his way into Syria and Cilicia, but he had never been seen by the "churches of Judaea," meaning the big established churches like the one in Jerusalem. This seems strange to us today. To our way of thinking, if Paul had wanted to be recognized anywhere it would have been in the "First Church" of the big city, the capital. Most young preachers today want to be known by the powers that be, to become associated with and recognized by the big names in important places. Yet here was Paul who was personally ordained and commissioned by the Lord Jesus Himself, and he went about launching his ministry in an out-of-the-way place like Damascus, not even bothering to try to make himself known outside his small area of influence.

That's the way it should be done. God may call you to some great ministry some day, but if He does, more than likely, He will start you out in that ministry in a small way. You may find yourself working for the Lord in some backwater area far away from where everything important seems to be happening. Why is that? It's part of God's management trainee program.

Before He gives you a great ministry, He will give you a small one. Once you have proven yourself in the small things, then you will be prepared for the larger. In our Father's business, there is always a proving time before promotion time.

If that happens to you, don't become discouraged. If you have what it takes, you'll get there. Advancement will come, but only when you're ready for it. Show yourself to be faithful and diligent where you are now, and when the time is right, God will reward that faithfulness and diligence by promoting you to a position of greater responsibility. The more responsible you prove yourself to be now, the more responsibility you will receive later on. Like it or not, that's just God's way: "And whosoever of you will be the chiefest, shall be servant of all" (Mark 10:44).

David tended sheep for years before he ever went out and slew Goliath. Do you know what he did after he had slain the giant? He went right back to tending sheep. You would have thought he would have been appointed governor of the land or at least captain of the armies of Israel. Of course, all that and more would come later. It wasn't his time. David wasn't elevated right away because he wasn't ready for it. He wasn't through growing yet.

The same is true of the prophet Elijah. We know nothing of Elijah's younger days. He just seemed to pop up on the scene when he was about thirty years old. Apparently he had spent those first thirty years of his life proving himself for the task that lay ahead of him. As is so often the case, it took Elijah years of preparation and effort to become an overnight success.

The same is true of Joseph. Joseph proved himself again and again: in his father's household, in the household of Potiphar, in the prison to which he had been wrongly sentenced. Whatever his circumstances, Joseph worked to show himself worthy of trust and responsibility, and he got them both, so much so that one day he was promoted to second in the land under Pharaoh himself. Another "overnight success."

Then there is our Lord Jesus Christ. God's own Son spent the first thirty of His thirty-three years of earthly life in obscurity, known only to a handful of people. But He was known to God. That's all that mattered, because in the fullness of time (when the time was just right) He was revealed for who He was (Matthew 3:17).

Think about that for a moment. For the first thirty years of His life, few had ever heard of Jesus of Nazareth. Now how many millions of people down through the ages have heard of Him? In three short years, Jesus went from the obscurity of a Galilean carpenter shop to becoming the very center of all human history.

So it will be with you if you are faithful. You will be revealed for who and what you are if you will stand behind the Word of God. Don't exalt yourself; exalt the Word: "Exalt her [wisdom], and she shall promote thee: she shall bring thee to honour, when thou dost embrace her" (Proverbs 4:8). If you want to be promoted, you must be worthy of promotion.

Many Christians are not prosperous today simply because they can't be trusted. God won't give them more money because they aren't faithful with what they have now. If the Lord can't trust a person with a hundred dollars, why would He give him a thousand? He would only squander it, waste it on his own pleasures and lusts. God entrusts His finest blessings to those who know how to handle them: "For whosoever hath, to him shall be given; and whosoever hath not, from him shall be taken even that which he seemeth to have" (Luke 8:18). The same principle that applies to possessions also applies to power and position: Responsibility begets responsibility.

1:24 And they glorified God in me.

The *New American Standard* Bible translation of this verse reads: "And they were glorifying God because of me." Paul did not seek after glory or fame or power or riches. He just preached the gospel to everyone he could, right where he was. As a result, his message spread throughout the Jewish world so even those in Jerusalem and the other great cities who did not know him by face knew him by report. Wherever he went, Paul's reputation preceded him. Why did that happen? Not because he was so handsome or intelligent or such a gifted preacher. It was not because he had such a dynamic personality. It happened because Paul put Jesus Christ at the center of his ministry: "For I determined not to know any thing among you, save Jesus Christ, and him crucified" (1 Corinthians 2:2).

Paul brought glory to God and, for that reason, God saw to it that glory came to Paul. That's the way it will be in your ministry as well. Just be faithful to preach the Word, and sooner or later you will come to be known by name and face just as Paul was.

V. The Jerusalem Incident (2:1–10)

As I have said, the book of Galatians has a dual theme: 1) salvation by the grace of God versus salvation by works, and 2) spirituality by grace versus spirituality by works. Both of these themes will be brought out in chapter 2 of Galatians. The first of these is illustrated by the incident in Jerusalem that Paul relates to the churches in Galatia.

2:1 ¶ Then after fourteen years I went up again to Jerusalem with Barnabas, and also took Titus with *me*.

Then fourteen years after [later] I went up again to Jerusalem . . .

In this verse, Paul reveals this was his second trip to Jerusalem after his conversion. The first was three years after he went to see Peter and spent two weeks with him, during which time he also saw James the brother of Jesus, but none of the other apostles. Now this second trip comes fourteen years after the first. In this passage, Paul reveals to us the reason for this second journey.

. . . with Barnabas, and took Titus with me also.

This statement is significant because Titus is the key person in this story, which we also find in the fifteenth chapter of Acts in which Paul and Barnabas defend their ministry before the church in Jerusalem. "And I went up by revelation, and communicated unto them [the church in Jerusalem] that gospel which I preach among the Gentiles" (v. 2).

Now we begin to get an understanding of Paul's reason for going back to Jerusalem. He told us he went there purposely to explain to them the gospel message he had been preaching to the Gentiles. Why, after all these years, did he suddenly decide he needed to go to Jerusalem to explain and defend his ministry? The answer has to do with what Paul perceived as a growing menace to the gospel of grace that he was defending to the Galatians in this chapter.

With the passage of time, the church in Jerusalem had begun to become very legalistic. It had originally come into being as a result of the thousands who came to the Lord through the preaching of the disciples on and after the day of Pentecost. Jerusalem had become the center of Christian missionary activity as evangelists were sent out in all directions to carry the good news. But as the site of the Jewish temple and the center of Hebrew culture, Jerusalem was also a hotbed of Judaism, which had infiltrated the church there through the years. Just as this situation came to a head, Paul received word by revelation of the Lord to make a journey back to the Jerusalem church. The timing of that revelation was no accident.

For over fourteen years, Paul had never gone to the Jerusalem church to tell them face-to-face of his ministry and message. What the believers in Jerusalem knew of him and his ministry had come back to them as hearsay. Only James and Peter had ever even talked to Paul firsthand (Galatians 1:18–19). Now he was to arrive on the scene at a crucial moment, bringing with him one of his Gentile converts — an action that was bound to bring matters to a head, as Paul no doubt knew full well. As a result of this confrontation, Judaism was set back for a time in the capital city, though it later resurfaced as it did from time to time and as legalism has always done throughout the centuries.

I believe it was at the time of his sojourn in Arabia that the Lord revealed to Paul His marvelous plan of salvation which he wrote about from then on, until the end of his life on earth. If that is true, Paul's remarks to the Galatians underline his motive for taking Barnabas, and especially Titus, with him on his return trip to Jerusalem to share his revelation with the church there. As a Gentile convert to Christ, being uncircumcised, Titus would be a living example (as well as a test case) of the doctrine of salvation by grace rather than by keeping of the Jewish law. So Titus' presence with Paul was not at all incidental; it was the real crux of his visit to the Jerusalem church. If Titus was accepted by the brothers in Jerusalem, it would stand as irrefutable evidence of the validity of Paul's apostleship and of his message of salvation by grace alone.

2:2 And I went up by revelation, and communicated to them that gospel which I preach among the Gentiles, but privately to those who were of reputation, lest by any means I might run, or had run, in vain.

Paul's visit to Jerusalem was not mere happenstance; it was divinely planned and timed. At just the right moment the Lord spoke to Paul and told him what to do to bring his message of grace to the home church.

. . . but privately to them which were of reputation . . .

"Them which were of reputation" were Peter, James, and John, the leaders in the Jerusalem church. Paul was very diplomatic and wise. Prior to taking his message before the entire church body, he arranged a private meeting with the church leaders to communicate to them what he had been preaching to the Gentiles and the results of that message.

. . . lest by any means I should run, or had run, in vain.

By this expression Paul was simply saying, "I was aware if I didn't handle this situation very carefully, I could destroy everything I was doing and had already done up to that time." That, too, is a lesson for us, especially those of us in the ministry.

It is highly important how we handle ourselves when dealing with others, both in the church and without. We might have the right message, the right words from God, but if we don't present them in the right manner, we could destroy our ministry. While I appreciate the implied integrity of those who continually boast of how they always preach the uncompromised Word, I must point out that there is a real danger in that attitude, the danger of spiritual pride.

Pride will destroy our witness faster than compromise any day. Nowhere is humility, tact, diplomacy, discretion, and wisdom needed more than when presenting the glorious gospel of the Lord Jesus Christ.

We must always be on guard against the dogmatism that so easily slips in to twist our message of love, grace, and forgiveness into one of ridicule and judgment of those who do not see things as we do. Although we cherish the right to preach the truth as we believe God has revealed it to us, we must never abuse that privilege by mistaking it as a license to impose our beliefs and convictions on others. We do well to always remember that none of us has an exclusive franchise on truth.

2:3 Yet not even Titus who *was* with me, being a Greek, was compelled to be circumcised.

Paul's meeting with the three leaders of the church was a success. By receiving his Gentile convert without requiring him to submit to the demands of Jewish circumcision, they were in essence endorsing Paul's message and ministry. This point is of vital importance, which is why Paul pointed it out to the believers in Galatia, themselves Gentiles, who therefore could identify with Titus.

2:4 And *this occurred* because of false brethren secretly brought in (who came in by stealth to spy out our liberty which we have in Christ Jesus, that they might bring us into bondage),

The *New International Version* says, "This matter arose because some false brothers had infiltrated our ranks to spy on the freedom we have in Christ Jesus and to make us slaves." Paul's victory was not to be won easily.

Somehow "false brethren," legalistic Judaizers, heard of Paul's meeting with the church leaders and came to challenge him before the elders. Paul used Titus to convince all who were present that salvation and spirituality were by faith alone. Since they could not beat Paul in conference (face-to-face), Paul's opponents began to follow his ministry and to undermine him privately after he left a city so he would not be there to defend himself or his message. This was exactly what happened in Galatia.

What was their ultimate purpose? "To make us slaves." That is the way legalism works. It always tries to bring into bondage those who have been set free by the gospel.

> **2:5 to whom we did not yield submission even for an hour, that the truth of the gospel might continue with you.**

The *New American Standard* Bible clarifies Paul's meaning in this verse, which it translates: "But we did not yield in subjection to them for even an hour, so that the truth of the gospel might remain with you." Paul was not fooled by these people for a minute, nor was he intimidated by them. He stood his ground against them and their attempts to bring him and his followers into subjection to legalism. Paul did this openly before all the church leaders of Jerusalem.

> **2:6–10 But from those who seemed to be something—whatever they were, it makes no difference to me; God shows personal favoritism to no man—for those who seemed *to be something* added nothing to me. 7 But on the contrary, when they saw that the gospel for the uncircumcised had been committed to me, as *the gospel* for the circumcised *was* to Peter 8 (for He who worked effectively in Peter for the apostleship to the circumcised also worked effectively in me toward the Gentiles),**
>
> **9 and when James, Cephas, and John, who seemed to be pillars, perceived the grace that had been given to me, they gave me and Barnabas the right hand of fellowship, that we *should go* to the Gentiles and they to the circumcised. 10 *They desired* only that we should remember the poor, the very thing which I also was eager to do.**

Let's read it in the *New International Version* to be sure we get Paul's message to the Galatians:

> 6 As for those who were held in high esteem—whatever they were makes no difference to me; God does not show favoritism—they added nothing to my message. 7 On the contrary, they recognized that I had been entrusted with the task of preaching the gospel to the uncircumcised, just as Peter had been to the circumcised. 8 For God, who was at work in Peter as an apostle to the circumcised, was also at work in me as an apostle to the Gentiles. 9 James, Cephas and John, those esteemed as pillars, gave me and Barnabas the right hand of fellowship when they recognized the grace given to me. They agreed that we should go to the Gentiles, and they to the circumcised. 10 All they asked was that we should continue to remember the poor, the very thing I had been eager to do all along. —NIV

So Paul was fully recognized and accepted as an apostle by the church in Jerusalem, which also endorsed his message of salvation by grace. They made no attempt to impose any restrictions whatsoever on Paul or his ministry or upon his Gentile convert, though it was fully known that Titus was an uncircumcised Greek. Thus, Paul related this Jerusalem incident to the believers in Galatia to impress upon them his full and complete vindication before the church fathers in Jerusalem and to emphasize to these people the completeness of their salvation by grace through simple faith in Jesus Christ and His finished work at Calvary.

The Jerusalem incident (vv. 1–10) illustrates Paul's theme of salvation by grace. In the remaining half of this chapter (vv. 11–17), his second theme, spirituality by grace, will be emphasized.

2:11–17 The Law

Thus far in our study of Galatians, we have seen that the book was written by Paul to the churches in Galatia to warn them about the legalistic Judaizers who had come into their midst to try to get them bound up in a system of law to which they as Gentiles had never been subject. This seems to have been a continual problem with which Paul had to contend throughout his ministry. Wherever he went, his greatest opposition was not from the paganistic Romans or the hedonistic Greeks, but from the legalistic Jews — his own countrymen. Even though they were born again, they still could not free themselves (and would not free others) from what they perceived to be the righteous demands of the law.

Incidentally, this constant aggravation and harassment is what I believe to be Paul's "thorn in the flesh" (2 Corinthians 12:7). No physical infirmity or affliction could have possibly dogged Paul's steps and caused him more torment than this religious "spirit" that plagued him at every turn for the rest of his earthly life and ministry.

We have said a great deal thus far about the law, but what exactly is it? And why did it pose such a hindrance and obstacle to the message of grace Paul preached wherever he went? There are five basic aspects of the Mosaic law we will consider here before continuing our study of the second chapter of Galatians. We are going to consider the Mosaic law carefully because it has had such a profound effect upon our own religious thinking even today. Whether most Christians realize it or not, our New Testament viewpoint and attitude (and thus our actions) are to a very real degree determined by an Old Testament legal system that was fulfilled and put away at the cross of Calvary, thus setting us free to live a whole new way of life.

I. Points about the Law

A. Mosaic Law Found in the First Five Books of the Bible

The entire content of what was referred to by the ancient Hebrews as "the law" was contained in only five books of the Old Testament: Genesis, Exodus, Leviticus, Numbers, and Deuteronomy. The Ten Commandments are not the entire Jewish law, but neither is the whole of the Old Testament part of that law. When the Lord commanded Joshua in Joshua 1:8 that this "book of the law" was not to depart out of his mouth, He was referring only to the first five books of the Old Testament. This was all of the Bible that had been written up to that time.

In Matthew 5:17, when the Lord Jesus indicated that He had come not "to destroy the law, or the prophets . . . but to fulfil" them, He was referring to the entire Old Testament: the law being the first five books of that body of holy writings, and the prophets, the major and minor prophets, comprising the rest of it. We need to remember that distinction in our consideration of the old covenant, which our savior came to fulfill on our behalf. Jesus fulfilled every law and prophecy of the Old Testament written about Him.

The law is divided into three categories:

1. The Moral Law

The moral law is comprised of the Ten Commandments. This body of rules and regulations was never intended as a means of salvation or spirituality for God's people. Then what was its purpose? Paul told us this in Romans 3:19–22:

> 19 Now we know that whatever the law says, it says to those who are under the law, that every mouth may be stopped, and all the world may become guilty before God. 20 Therefore by the deeds of the law no flesh will be justified in His sight, for by the law is the knowledge of sin. 21 But now the righteousness of God apart from the law is revealed, being witnessed by the Law and the Prophets, 22 even the righteousness of God, through faith in Jesus Christ, to all and on all who believe. For there is no difference; —Romans 3:19–22

The purpose of the moral law was to show man he is a sinner and in need of a Savior. It was given as an unattainable standard of absolute perfection so men would realize their need of accepting God's free gift of righteousness through faith. That's why legalism is so damnable. By striving for perfection through self-effort, it attempts to circumvent the very plan of salvation that God Himself established from the beginning — which was salvation by grace and not by works.

Even in the Old Testament, salvation, God's righteousness, came without the law. Faith has always been the means of salvation and spirituality. This was manifested and witnessed by the law and the prophets. The law taught salvation by grace. Every sacrifice pointed to Jesus and away from man. Every prophet taught salvation by grace and told of the coming of the Lord Jesus, the only one who could redeem mankind.

No one, no matter how pure or devout he may be, can ever attain salvation through self-effort. The only way to attain salvation is to be born again. Spirituality afterward comes as we live by the Spirit. Not only does the moral law not lead to salvation, it doesn't even lead to spirituality. It is impossible to live the Ten Commandments in the natural. The only way to keep the commandments is in the supernatural. A person must be born again to even fulfill the moral code.

Can you see then why no one up until the time of Jesus could keep the law? The law could not be kept before the resurrection of Jesus Christ from the dead because no one had yet been born again. No one had ever had the Holy Spirit imparted into their human spirit to re-create them and fill them with supernatural power. Can you also see why, after the day of Pentecost, the law was put away forever?

You and I are no longer under the law. Jesus Christ fulfilled the law for us. We are under a new dispensation called *grace* because we live, not by a set of rules and regulations carved in stone, but by the supernatural infilling presence and power of God's own Holy Spirit. Therefore as we walk in that Spirit, we keep the law. The Spirit leads us in love, and we keep all God's laws whether we realize it or not. Love is the fulfilling of the law (Galatians 5:14).

2. Shadow Christology

The second part of the law included the sacrifices, temple furniture, feast days, and rituals of Jewish ceremonial worship. Its purpose was to symbolize the fulfillment of the moral law. That fulfillment was Christ.

First the Jewish law presented the problem: no one could be saved by the law because no one could keep it. The law was like a chain with ten links in it. To break any one of those links was to break the entire chain (See James 2:10). That's why the people had to constantly bring sacrifices to the temple to atone for their sin in breaking the law. Life under the old system was a vicious cycle of breaking the law and making sacrifice for being a lawbreaker.

1 For the law, having a shadow of the good things to come, and not the very image of the things, can never with these same sacrifices, which they offer continually year by year, make those who approach perfect. 2 For then would they not have ceased to be offered? For the worshipers, once purified, would have had no more consciousness of sins. 3 But in those sacrifices there

is a reminder of sins every year. 4 For it is not possible that the blood of bulls and goats could take away sins. —Hebrews 10:1–4

As the writer of Hebrews pointed out, this continual process did not permanently remove sin, the sin nature, or sin consciousness. On the contrary, it served only as a constant reminder to the people of their sinfulness. This was what it was designed to do, to make the people aware they were sinners in constant need of redemption and unable to redeem themselves.

Second, the law presented the solution to that problem: there would one day come a savior who would fulfill the righteous requirements of the law for all those who would put their faith in Him.

11 But Christ came as High Priest of the good things to come, with the greater and more perfect tabernacle not made with hands, that is, not of this creation. 12 Not with the blood of goats and calves, but with His own blood He entered the Most Holy Place once for all, having obtained eternal redemption. —Hebrews 9:11–12

Under the old system, every time the people made sacrifice for their sin, it pointed to the coming of the Lord Jesus who would one day put away that law forever (because it was imperfect, being conditioned and dependent on man who was himself imperfect and fallible). This system was just a shadow of the real sacrifice to come. The ritualistic elements of Jewish worship all had a meaning. They symbolized the death, burial, and resurrection of the promised Messiah, the Savior of Israel, the Lord Jesus Christ.

Whether the worship ritual involved a grain offering, offering of wine or oil, bringing of the firstfruits to the altar, or the blood sacrifice of a dove, lamb, or oxen, it always portrayed one thing: the atonement, the sacrifice of the life of the Savior for His people. Thus the whole ceremonial system evolved around and centered on blood. Why? To continually remind the people of the blood of the Anointed One that would be shed for the remission of their sin.

3. The Social Law

The third part of the law had to do with dietary regulations, rules of sanitation, and instructions on the proper care of land and crops. Like the first part, this was also fulfilled by part two, the coming of the Messiah. He fulfilled the moral law and the social law by His perfect life, but He fulfilled the shadow Christology by His death, resurrection, and ascension into heaven to sit at the right hand of God the Father.

B. The Law was Given to Israel Only

And Moses went up to God, and the Lord called to him from the mountain, saying, "Thus you shall say to the house of Jacob, and tell the children of Israel: —Exodus 19:3

These are the statutes and judgments and laws which the Lord made between Himself and the children of Israel on Mount Sinai by the hand of Moses. —Leviticus 26:46

Now we know that whatever the law says, it says to those who are under the law, that every mouth may be stopped, and all the world may become guilty before God. —Romans 3:19

Who are Israelites, to whom pertain the adoption, the glory, the covenants, the giving of the law, the service of God, and the promises; —Romans 9:4

If the law was to the house of Jacob, the children of Israel, to whom Moses gave the statutes and judgments and laws, then it stands to reason that these statutes and judgments and laws were not given to Gentiles:

For what nation is there so great, who hath God so nigh unto them, as the LORD our God is in all things that we call upon him for? —Deuteronomy 4:7

12 For as many as have sinned without law will also perish without law, and as many as have sinned in the law will be judged by the law 13 (for not the hearers of the law are just in the sight of God, but the doers of the law will be justified; 14 for when Gentiles, who do not have the law, by nature do the things in the law, these, although not having the law, are a law to themselves, —Romans 2:12–14

C. Christians are not under the Mosaic Law

For sin shall not have dominion over you, for you are not under law but under grace. —Romans 6:14

For I through the law died to the law that I might live to God. —Galatians 2:19

Since we Christians are Gentiles and not Jews, we are not under the Jewish law. Jesus Christ fulfilled that law for us two thousand years before our birth. Why then should we be bound by it today? We aren't. That's the good news of the gospel, that Jesus Christ fulfilled all the law. When He said on the cross, "It is finished," He was not referring to the plan of salvation because that would not be completed until He had ascended to the Father. He was referring to the Mosaic law He had come to fulfill (Matthew 5:17). Now because that law is completely fulfilled, but you and I are under a higher law, "the law of the Spirit of life in Christ Jesus," which has made us free from "the law of sin and death" (Romans 8:2).

Since Jesus Christ fulfilled the law for us long ago, the only way you and I can fulfill the law today is to believe in Him and have His perfect life, His righteousness, imputed to us. We did that when we accepted Him into our life. We received everything He did on the cross. He did all the work for us. He earned the righteousness, He won the salvation, and He merited the grace, for us. We did nothing but receive it all by faith.

The law tried to produce life from the outside in, but the weakness of the law was in the flesh. The reason the law could never succeed is because all men have the nature of flesh, and that carnal nature can never please God: "So then they that are in the flesh cannot please God" (Romans 8:8). The way Jesus Christ produced life was from the inside out. He recreated our human spirits. When a person listens to the dictates of the human spirit guided by the Holy Spirit, which he has received through Christ, the flesh must line up and the law is kept in him by the power of the Holy Spirit.

Some people, hearing me preach this message, say to me: "You're teaching Christians are not supposed to keep the law."

"Well, yes and no," I tell them. "No, we don't have to go back and try to keep the law. But yes, we do keep it."

As a Christian, I don't break the law. Do you know why not? I walk after the Spirit, and according to Paul, those who walk after the Spirit fulfill the law (Romans 8:1).

"Yes," these people say, "but if God put the Ten Commandments in the Bible, I think we ought to try to keep them."

"Well, if you think the Ten Commandments are so important," I say to them, "then quote them to me."

Naturally they can't. They might get a few, but very seldom all of them, and almost never in order.

"I don't understand that," I say. "You think you ought to be keeping something you don't even know well enough to quote correctly."

I follow the Ten Commandments. I live up to virtually all of them all the time, but I never learned to quote them. And I don't really care that I can't. I walk in the Spirit, not by law. Because I walk in the Spirit, I find myself doing those things that please the Spirit. I walk in love, and according to our Lord, love is the fulfillment of all the law (Matthew 22:37–40).

Although we Christians are not under the law, we do keep it. We keep it the same way Jesus did. Can you imagine our Lord walking along beside the Sea of Galilee worrying about whether He had broken any of the commandments that day? No, I don't think He ever did that. He didn't strive to keep the law. He just walked in the Spirit, and therefore did not fulfill the lust of the flesh. By not fulfilling the lust of the flesh, He kept the law. That's the way you and I keep it. By following the Holy Spirit who is in us.

Walking in the Spirit produces life from the inside out. It produces the fruit of the Spirit: "love, joy, peace, longsuffering, gentleness, goodness, faith, meekness, temperance: against such there is no law" (Galatians 5:23–24).

D. Today the Law Applies Only to the Unbeliever

> 9 knowing this: that the law is not made for a righteous person, but for the lawless and insubordinate, for the ungodly and for sinners, for the unholy and profane, for murderers of fathers and murderers of mothers, for manslayers, 10 for fornicators, for sodomites, for kidnappers, for liars, for perjurers, and if there is any other thing that is contrary to sound doctrine, —1 Timothy 1:9–10

Does the law have any significance today? Only to the unbeliever, the unregenerate person. He is the only one affected by it. The law is still there to do for him what it did for those under it, to point out the need for a savior.

For us who have already received that savior, we are no longer under the law but under grace. One day all the unregenerate will be judged by the law, according to their works (cf. Matthew 25:31–46, Revelation 20:12–15). But to those of us who are in Christ Jesus, there is no condemnation, no judgment. We have already passed from death unto life (cf. Romans 8:1, 1 John 3:14).

E. The Law Has Limitations

In the book of Galatians, Paul points out four limitations of the law:

1. It Cannot Justify

Knowing that a man is not justified by the works of the law but by faith in Jesus Christ, even we have believed in Christ Jesus, that we might be justified by faith in Christ and not by the works of the law; for by the works of the law no flesh shall be justified. —Galatians 2:16

2. It Cannot Give Life

Is the law then against the promises of God? Certainly not! For if there had been a law given which could have given life, truly righteousness would have been by the law. —Galatians 3:21

3. It Cannot Provide the Holy Spirit

This only I want to learn from you: Did you receive the Spirit by the works of the law, or by the hearing of faith? —Galatians 3:2

4. It Cannot Produce Miracles

Therefore He who supplies the Spirit to you and works miracles among you, does He do it by the works of the law, or by the hearing of faith? —Galatians 3:5

This last point is very important: the law cannot produce miracles. Think about that for a moment. If you have been in Pentecostal circles for very many years, you can recall when meetings were marked by numerous and tremendous miracles. Yet today such miracles happen less often in many churches. Why is that? What has happened to stifle the flow of God's power? Very simply, what we are seeing today is the result of legalism.

At first ministers were preaching only from God's Word, and God responded by pouring out His Spirit and by confirming the Word preached with signs following. However, somewhere along the line, the classical Pentecostals began to turn away from the preaching of the Word to the preaching of rules, regulations, and codes of dress and speech and behavior. They got caught up in deciding things like sleeve length and dress length. They turned their attention from proclaiming the gospel of freedom to denouncing card playing, lipstick wearing, and moviegoing. So the power of God was cut off.

Today there is a new revival of miracles and healings in these latter days. Do you know why? We've gotten away from preaching all the dos and don'ts and started preaching the Word again. The miracles and signs and wonders have begun to occur once again, but do you know the amazing thing about all this? Spirit-filled people still dress and speak and behave modestly. The Word in their life sets the standard.

Some preachers seem to be afraid that if they don't constantly remind their people of all these rules and regulations, they will get completely out of hand and start doing anything they want to. My answer to them is, "Preach the Word and let your people make up their own minds. You'll be amazed at what the liberating gospel of Jesus Christ does to people. Once they learn they are truly free to do what they want to, they seem to realize what they want to do is follow the Spirit of the Lord."

This is precisely why the Lord wants that gospel preached. He wants His children to obey out of hearts of love and appreciation for all He has done for them in Christ, not because they're browbeaten and coerced into doing right or because they're afraid not to behave. Preach the gospel and people will receive the Spirit. Then when the Spirit moves, people will follow Him, not out of a sense of duty or obligation or guilt, but willingly and joyfully because where the Spirit is, there is joy and peace and liberty.

With that understanding of the law, let's now look at the second of the two incidents Paul describes in chapter 2. Keep in mind he was writing to emphasize to them the sufficiency of God's grace to save to the uttermost those who come to Him not by the law but through Jesus Christ His son (Hebrews 7:25).

II. The Antioch Incident (11–17)

Before we get into this story in detail, let's back up a little and set the stage for what is happening in these verses. As stated previously, some time after its initial beginnings on the day of Pentecost, the church in Jerusalem began to go downhill (as churches do when they start to become legalistic). The Spirit of the Lord simply began to move away from Jerusalem to find another place in which He could minister freely. He found that place in Antioch where He raised up a new church that was not preaching dos and don'ts.

Most of the members of the church were Gentiles and knew nothing of the Jewish law. Therefore, these people were free to preach the gospel and worship God in spirit and truth. All they knew was the Word of the Lord brought to them by Paul on one of his missionary journeys. Since all they had to go by was the New Testament teaching of salvation by grace, this church was able to flourish and missionaries went out everywhere to spread the good news of Jesus Christ.

In time, the church in Jerusalem, which by now considered itself the headquarters of Christianity, heard about what was happening in Antioch and immediately became jealous of its apparent success. Because the church in Antioch was made up of Gentiles and had been established by Paul, naturally the Jews in Jerusalem were not at all sure about its orthodoxy. After all, it had never received their seal of approval. In light of the situation, they decided they had better send a representative to Antioch to investigate and report back to them his findings.

Since Peter was one of the founders of the Jerusalem church and a devout Jew of good standing, they chose him as their envoy to Antioch. He made his way there where he soon became involved in the affairs of the local church, so involved, in fact, he remained longer than necessary. The church in Jerusalem became concerned enough to send others to find out exactly what was going on. This time they sent a team of legalistic Jews. It was the arrival of this group of Jewish believers from Jerusalem that sparked the incident in Antioch described by Paul in this passage.

This passage highlights spirituality by grace.

> **2:11 ⸿ Now when Peter had come to Antioch, I withstood him to his face, because he was to be blamed;**

This word translated "withstood" is from a Greek word meaning to resist or to oppose. So this very Paul whom the home church in Jerusalem knew so little about and generally mistrusted has the nerve to speak out publicly against the great apostle Peter (whom many Christians today look upon as the first leader of the church). Why does Paul oppose Peter? "Because he was to be blamed" (v. 11). Paul opposes Peter because he is doing wrong.

2:12 for before certain men came from James, he would eat with the Gentiles; but when they came, he withdrew and separated himself, fearing those who were of the circumcision.

While in Antioch, Peter ate and drank with the Gentiles there, which was expressly forbidden to devout Jews under the law. What do you think Peter ate with the Gentiles? Surely their menu contained many foods that were forbidden to a Jew under the law, but Peter knew he was no longer under the law. He knew it because the Lord had revealed it to him through the vision He gave him when He sent him to preach the gospel to Cornelius and his family who were Gentiles:

> Then he said to them, "You know how unlawful it is for a Jewish man to keep company with or go to one of another nation. But God has shown me that I should not call any man common or unclean. —Acts 10:28

Peter knew better than to separate himself from non-Jews. Then why did he do it? Because he was "fearing them which were of the circumcision" (Galatians 2:12). Peter withdrew from his freedom as a Christian and subjected himself to the dictates of the Jewish law for only one reason, fear. As long as he was alone with the Gentiles, he ate and drank and fellowshipped with them freely. But as soon as the group sent by James from the Jerusalem church arrived on the scene, Peter became worried about what they would think of his actions.

This is curious because Peter had already settled this issue of consorting with Gentiles in the very Jerusalem church from which these men had been sent. When news about Peter's trip to preach to Cornelius and his family got back to the church in Jerusalem, they called Peter in to explain what he was doing in going to the Gentiles. We read about this incident and Peter's response in Acts 11:1–18:

¹ Now the apostles and brethren who were in Judea heard that the Gentiles had also received the word of God. ² And when Peter came up to Jerusalem, those of the circumcision contended with him, ³ saying, "You went in to uncircumcised men and ate with them!" ⁴ But Peter explained it to them in order from the beginning, saying: . . . ¹⁸ When they heard these things they became silent; and they glorified God, saying, "Then God has also granted to the Gentiles repentance to life." —Acts 11:1–4, 18

Notice who it was who contended with Peter about his dealings with Gentiles: "they that were of the circumcision" (Acts 11:2). Now notice who had just arrived in Antioch to investigate matters there, the ones Paul said Peter was afraid of: "them which were of the circumcision."

Isn't it strange this same apostle, Peter, who stood before the whole church in Jerusalem to defend his actions in going in and eating with Gentiles should now be afraid to be seen doing the same thing by these very same people? That's one reason Paul became so angry with Peter. Peter knew better than to do what he was doing. Paul also knew Peter was leading others astray by his wrong attitude and actions.

2:13 And the rest of the Jews also played the hypocrite with him, so that even Barnabas was carried away with their hypocrisy.

And the other Jews dissembled likewise with him; insomuch that Barnabas also was carried away with their dissimulation.

This one little act of legalism split the whole church at Antioch right down the middle. One bit of leaven leavens the whole lump. This word translated "dissembled" is from a Greek word meaning to act hypocritically in concert with someone.

Who is it who acts hypocritically in this situation? The Jews. Who was the someone they act hypocritically in concert with? It was Peter, the great apostle, the very one who should have been taking the lead in promoting unity in the church (as he had done in the case of Cornelius and his family) instead of causing divisions.

Again, there is a lesson for us here. Just because we are not in total agreement with the doctrines or practices of other Christian churches does not mean we are to withdraw and separate ourselves from them. The biblical call to "come out . . . and be ye separate" (2 Corinthians 6:17) does not refer to separation from our brothers and sisters in Christ, regardless of their sectarian affiliation. Nothing is needed more in our society today than a united church of Jesus Christ. We need more and more churches (and individual Christians) coming together in a spirit of harmony and brotherhood.

How are we ever going to reach the world with our message of God's love and acceptance if we don't love and accept each other? Unity in Christ is part of the message of grace. To separate ourselves into little self-centered cliques is to dissemble, to act the hypocrite. God forbid that we Christians should ever join these self-righteous Jews in their dissimulation.

Notice, Paul emphasizes that even Barnabas has been influenced by Peter's actions. Why is it so important that Barnabas joined in with this dissimulation? Barnabas is the pastor of the church in Antioch. The pastor is supposed to be a bridge between the various elements of his church, not a cause of division. Any time a pastor gets personally involved in a church division, that church is destined to split. Paul stresses the importance of unity among the brethren by condemning the prime cause of division: *an attitude of exclusiveness.*

2:14 ¶ But when I saw that they were not straightforward about the truth of the gospel, I said to Peter before *them* all, "If you, being a Jew, live in the manner of Gentiles and not as the Jews, why do you compel Gentiles to live as Jews?

"Them all" refers to the members of the church in Antioch. Whereas Paul had met privately with the church leaders in Jerusalem before presenting his case before the church there, he showed no such discretion in this case. On the contrary, he stood up in front of the whole church body to denounce Peter for his wrongdoing.

This is not the way I would recommend handling problems in the church, but obviously Paul thought this case called for drastic measures. He took Peter to task openly, knowing that his remarks to him pertained to all the Jews in that crowd who had joined him in his wrongdoing. In this letter to the Galatians, he uses that incident as an object lesson to drive home his point of justification by grace and not by the keeping of the Jewish law.

Let's look at Paul's logic in his argument for justification by grace without regard to the law. He is saying to Peter, "You are a Jew, yet you have been living like a Gentile, just as though the Jewish law had no jurisdiction over you. If you, a Jew, are not subject to the Jewish law, then why are you trying to force the Gentiles to live by it?"

2:15 We *who are* Jews by nature, and not sinners of the Gentiles,

Here Paul included himself in his argument. "By nature" means by birth. And "not sinners of the Gentiles" is part of the expression of the old Jewish attitude that there were only two kinds of people in the world: Jews and sinners. (To the ancient Jews, the word "Gentile" meant heathen, one without God, a sinner.)

Paul uses this age-old Hebrew phrase to lead up to the point he made in chapter 3: *being born a Jew does not make a person the seed of Abraham and heir to the promises of God.* He will show the seed of Abraham is not a physical race, but a spiritual race. Therefore, the true Jew is not one who is circumcised physically, but one whose heart has been circumcised through the new birth. And the law is not that which is written on tablets of stone, but that which God has written on the hearts of those who have exercised the faith of Abraham. These are the true Jews.

2:16 knowing that a man is not justified by the works of the law but by faith in Jesus Christ, even we have believed in Christ Jesus, that we might be justified by faith in Christ and not by the works of the law; for by the works of the law no flesh shall be justified.

What did we say was the purpose of the law? To show man he was a sinner and incapable of attaining righteousness and salvation by his own efforts. The law was given to convince men of their need of a Savior. Its purpose was to bring man face-to-face with his own lack of righteousness so he would turn to God and receive the gift of His righteousness freely, through His Son Jesus Christ.

2:17 ¶ "But if, while we seek to be justified by Christ, we ourselves also are found sinners, *is* Christ therefore a minister of sin? Certainly not!

Paul used his debater technique in this verse to finally put a noose around Peter's neck. What Paul was saying to Peter here: "Peter, if you and I are trying to live a spiritual life before God by keeping the law, then we are saying it is the law that makes us spiritual after we are saved by grace. By your actions you are saying a person is saved by grace but in order to be spiritual, he must go back and keep the law.

"But what did the law do, Peter? Didn't it reveal you were a sinner? You were born again by faith in Christ Jesus. Now you are going back to the law that declares you to be a sinner! Do you know what that means? It means that Jesus Christ saved you to turn you into a sinner! You are telling these people that Jesus Christ is a minister of sin.That's blasphemy!"

Paul made it clear that the law is not the way to become spiritual. If a person is made worthy by faith in Jesus Christ, then it is by faith in Jesus Christ he is made spiritual. If he couldn't save himself by his own efforts, he cannot sanctify himself by his own efforts. Spirituality, like salvation, is a gift of God, not the result of works. This is the message Paul would have the Galatians learn. It is also the lesson he would have us learn today.

2:18–3:5 Grace Versus Works

I. The Word of Reconciliation

In our previous study, we noted that Paul recounts two incidents to the Galatians. The first incident, which took place in Jerusalem, served to point out the difference between the false concept of salvation by works and the gospel message of salvation by grace. The second of these two incidents, in Antioch, emphasized that spirituality, like salvation, is also a product of faith, "not of works, lest any man should boast" (Ephesians 2:9). No one is ever saved or justified by works of the law because the law is nothing more than a mirror to reflect a person's own unrighteousness and convince him of his need to receive God's free gift of redemption and righteousness.

No Christian ever has to work to become righteous; he is declared righteous by God. That's how he got saved. This is the basic concept Paul was trying to teach the Galatians so they would never again be deceived into trying to attain something by their own efforts that God had already given them by His grace.

This message is what Paul referred to in his second letter to the Corinthians as "the ministry of reconciliation; to wit, that God was in Christ, reconciling the world unto himself, not imputing their trespasses unto them" (2 Corinthians 5:18–19). The *New International Version* translates verse 19, "God was reconciling the world to himself in Christ, not counting men's sins against them." It is this "word of reconciliation" that Paul shares with these people in the churches of Galatia.

With this thought in mind, let's continue our study in the second chapter of his letter.

II. Crucified with Christ (18–21)

2:18 For if I build again those things which I destroyed, I make myself a transgressor.

When Paul speaks of building again the things that he destroyed, he was referring to going back to the law to seek justification. He says this because he knows when a person is born again, the law is destroyed in his life; it will never again be valid to him. As far as that person is concerned, the law is dead. To go back and try to resurrect it is to make himself a transgressor.

God never makes any person a transgressor. People do that to themselves. They do so by choosing the dead law over the living Lord, which is self-deception. It is bad enough for a person to allow someone else to deceive him; it's even worse to deceive himself.

2:19 For I through the law died to the law that I might live to God.

The law was not designed to give life; it was designed to kill. To attempt to achieve eternal life through the law is to commit suicide.

In 2 Corinthians 3:6, Paul wrote, "For the letter [of the law] killeth, but the spirit giveth life." The law kills. No one knows the truth of this statement better than Paul. Until his conversion on the road to Damascus, he had been a Pharisee, a Hebrew of the Hebrews, "touching the righteousness which is in the law, blameless" (Philippians 3:6). He knew what he was talking about when he said the law kills.

Once a person realizes he is dead, there is hope that he will turn to the Lord who alone can give him life. One purpose of the law is to kill so God can resurrect to eternal life. Paul recognizes this truth.

2:20 I have been crucified with Christ; it is no longer I who live, but Christ lives in me; and the *life* which I now live in the flesh I live by faith in the Son of God, who loved me and gave Himself for me.

This verse is not translated correctly in the *King James Version*. The phrase "I am crucified" should read, "I *have been* crucified." The Greek verb tense indicates that this is a past work that has already been completed. You and I are not in the state of being crucified, nor are we in a perpetual state of crucifixion. Like Christ, we were crucified once and for all time the moment we identified ourselves with His crucifixion and were born again of the Spirit of God. We died on the cross with our Lord. We were buried with Him in death. We were resurrected with Him to newness of life. We ascended with Him and now we are seated with Him in heavenly places (Ephesians 2:5–6).

Aren't you glad Jesus is not still on the cross? Neither are we. We don't have to go around daily crucifying our old man. He's dead. He was nailed to the cross. We have become brand new creatures: "Therefore if any man be in Christ, he is a new creature: old things are passed away; behold, all things are become new" (2 Corinthians 5:17). Just as Jesus never has to go to the cross to be crucified again, neither do we have to die again and again: "For the law of the Spirit of life in Christ Jesus hath made me [us] free from the law of sin and death" (Romans 8:2).

The expression "yet not I" is not found in the original Greek version of Galatians 2:20. This Scripture could better be translated: "I have been crucified with Christ, and I no longer live; but Christ lives in me."

Paul is saying the law killed him. What happens when a person dies? When someone dies, he is not annihilated. Death is never annihilation. Physical death is the separation of the inward man from the outward man. The inward man, the real man, either goes on to be with the Lord in heaven or to be with the devil in hell — one of the two. The outward shell of the person remains on the earth with nothing in it.

That's what happens when you and I are born again; our old natures inside us, that once belonged to Satan, moved out, and the Spirit of Jesus Christ came to live in our physical bodies. Our bodies didn't change. It wasn't the outward man that changed; it was the inward man who was born again. It is not so much our "old [spiritual] man" we must contend with now. It's the flesh that gives us so much trouble, and Satan who is at large in the earth. However, this is really no problem because greater is He who lives in us than he who is in the world (1 John 4:4). Therefore we can still overcome him by the blood of Jesus and the word of our testimony (Revelation 12:11).

"And the life which I now live (after the new birth) I live by faith in the Son of God, who loved me, and gave Himself for me." This translation brings out better the twofold theme of the book of Galatians: salvation by faith, spirituality by faith. Paul stresses the fact he was dead, crucified with Christ, then resurrected, born again by faith, and the life he now lives, after his salvation experience was also by faith. The life he lived in this fleshly body was not of the law; it was full of grace.

Our salvation is a free gift from God. We don't deserve it; we can't earn it. All we do to receive it is accept it by faith. In the same way, our spiritual life after salvation is by grace; we can never deserve or earn it by our own efforts. It, too, is a gift of God received by faith.

Does this mean we no longer need to pray or read the Bible or attend church or give offerings? Not to merit righteousness we don't. As good as all these things are, they won't merit righteousness any more than they would merit salvation. Then why do we do them? We do them because we want to, because we love God and want to communicate with Him, hear from Him, learn more about Him, serve Him, and have a part in His ministry of reconciliation. Any other reason for doing these things is selfish. It's legalistic. It's trying to get God to do something for us because we've done something for Him. That is the wrong motivation. We can never please God by our self-striving efforts.

Some people think they move God by their faith. That's not so. God has already moved by His grace. All we do is accept by our faith what God has already done.

I like to think of it this way. Grace is God reaching out toward us, and faith is us reaching out toward God. God reached out first, and we reach out second. Our faith does not cause God to move; His grace causes our faith to move. We are not saved because God responds to our faith and saves us. Redemption has been completed ever since Jesus Christ rose from the grave. The work is finished. God's part is done. That is grace. Now our part is accepting that which has already been done for us. That's faith. Faith does not move God to action. Faith is our action in response to God's grace. Grace always precedes faith.

We don't attain righteousness by our efforts. It was given to us by God as an act of His grace. Now we accept that righteousness by faith, by responding to what God has already done for us in Jesus Christ.

> **2:21 I do not set aside the grace of God; for if righteousness *comes* through the law, then Christ died in vain."**

I do not frustrate the grace of God: for if righteousness come by the law, then Christ is dead in vain.

This word translated "frustrate" actually means to nullify or to stop. Paul is saying "I do not nullify the grace of God by my self-efforts to attain righteousness; because if righteousness could be gained by works of the law, then Christ died for nothing."

III. Works of the Law or Hearing of Faith? (3:1–5)

> **3:1 ¶ O foolish Galatians! Who has bewitched you that you should not obey the truth, before whose eyes Jesus Christ was clearly portrayed among you as crucified?**

The word translated "foolish" is closer to our word *stupid*. "Bewitched" means hypnotized. What Paul is saying here is: "O you stupid Galatians, who has hypnotized you? The church in Jerusalem became hypnotized, and so did the one in Antioch. You have been deceived into falling into the same trap they did. Who is responsible for this deception?"

Of course, we know the answer to that question. It was the legalistic Judaizers who had come in after Paul's departure from Galatia to deceive the ignorant Galatians into giving up their freedom in Christ for bondage to a law to which they were never subject. Paul obviously had a hard time accepting that anyone would be so foolish as to fall for such a thing. He can only assume these clever Judaizers with their impressive credentials and shrewd arguments have managed to mesmerize these gullible Galatians by dangling the law in front of them.

. . . before whose eyes Jesus Christ hath been evidently set forth, crucified among you.

The problem with the Galatians is they have eye trouble. They move their eyes away from the truth to behold a lie. In so doing, they allow themselves to become blinded to the truth. They become so spellbound by the brilliance of the Judaizers and their smooth talk that they fall for their line. They had substituted the law of sin and death for the gospel of grace and life.

The word "evidently" here means clearly. Paul was saying to these people, "How could you have been so foolish as to take your eyes off Jesus Christ who was clearly portrayed in front of you, crucified, to turn them to the distortion of the law?"

3:2 This only I want to learn from you: Did you receive the Spirit by the works of the law, or by the hearing of faith?

This only would I learn of you . . .

Pauls is saying, "Just tell me one thing."

. . . Received ye the Spirit by the works of the law, or by the hearing of faith?"

Here he is asking, "Did you receive the Spirit of God by keeping the Jewish law, or by simply receiving Him by faith in Jesus Christ?"

Paul is not speaking of the baptism of the Spirit — of being filled with the Spirit — but simply of receiving the Spirit of God through the new birth. He was asking these people if they were born again of the Spirit by their own efforts or whether their redemption was a gift from God received by faith alone. The answer, of course, is the latter. As foolish as they were, the Galatians knew it was by grace they have been saved, through faith. They knew their redemption was not of themselves but was the gift of God: it was not of works, lest any of them should boast of having achieved it by his own efforts (Ephesians 2:8–9).

3:3 Are you so foolish? Having begun in the Spirit, are you now being made perfect by the flesh?

Paul wants to know this: "If you are saved by grace, then why are you now trying to be sanctified by works? If you began your new life by being born of the Spirit, why are you now trying to live that new life by your own efforts? Are you really so stupid you don't realize you remain spiritual the same way you became spiritual — by faith in Jesus Christ?"

3:4 Have you suffered so many things in vain—if indeed *it was* in vain?

Paul is asking the Galatians, "Have you suffered all these trials and tribulations for nothing? Tribulation came to you for your faith. Your faith carried you through, not the law. After successfully coming through many battles, are you now going to turn to the law? It wasn't your self-efforts at keeping the law that brought opposition against you neither was it keeping the law that brought you through the opposition. It was your faith in Jesus Christ that both made you the target of the evil one and gave you victory over him. Are you now ready to give up that 'faith which was once delivered unto the saints' (Jude 3), that faith for which you so earnestly contended, to turn back to dead works of the law?"

Some Christians don't understand the connection between faith and persecution. Either they think having faith exempts a person from all trials and tribulation, or they go to the opposite extreme and think that trials and tribulation are sent by God to test their faith. Neither of these two extreme views is accurate. Christians are not exempt from persecution, but persecution is not from God. Jesus warned that in this world we would have tribulation (John 16:33). But He also told us why tribulation would come upon us: "Persecution ariseth for the word's sake" (Mark 4:17). He further told us the source of that tribulation: "The thief cometh not, but for to steal, and to kill, and to destroy" (John 10:10).

Christians will face trials and tribulation in this world. We will be persecuted for the Word's sake. But this persecution is not sent by God to test our faith. Rather it is sent by Satan to destroy our faith. That's why it is so important that we "earnestly contend for the faith which was once delivered unto the saints" (Jude 3). By so doing, we grow in faith and power. But it is not persecution that makes us strong; it is the faith we use in that persecution that strengthens us.

As we increase in physical and spiritual prosperity, we increase the likelihood of becoming the target of Satan's attacks. Some people don't realize that prosperity and persecution go together. Didn't Jesus promise His disciples that along with the "hundredfold return" there would also be a similar increase in persecution (Mark 10:30)? Although Jesus warned them that in this world there would be tribulation, He also exhorted them not to be afraid because He had overcome the world.

Tribulation always ends in victory for the faithful child of God. That's why Paul reproves these Galatians for being so foolish as to abandon the faith for which they had contended in order to turn back to the law that has no power to defeat the enemy.

3:5 ¶ Therefore He who supplies the Spirit to you and works miracles among you, *does He do it* by the works of the law, or by the hearing of faith?

Paul is speaking of himself in this verse, referring to the first time he came to Galatia to establish these churches to which he is now writing. He is modestly pointing out that the one who worked miracles in their midst (Paul himself) did so by the presence and power of the Holy Spirit within him, and not by works of the law. The law cannot produce miracles any more than it can give the new birth.

Are miracles worked by the Spirit of God, or by the law? Do healings take place as a consequence of the teaching of the law or as a result of the preaching of the message of faith? The answer to these questions should not be hard to recognize, even for these blinded Galatians.

As we have noted, legalism cannot produce miracles. It is the preaching of the Word, not the teaching of rules and regulations, that God confirms with miracles, signs, and wonders! That's why I am determined to preach the Word of God from cover to cover. Other ministers may do as they will, but I am going to hold forth the message of faith, because I know it is by the hearing of faith miracles are wrought. The Word of God never changes. "Jesus Christ is the same yesterday, and today, and for ever" (Hebrews 13:8).

3:6–10 Abraham's Gospel

I. The Righteousness of Abraham (6)

3:6 just as Abraham *"believed God, and it was accounted to him for righteousness."*

Abraham was born, lived, and died before the law ever came into existence. Yet he was saved. And he was spiritual. If Abraham could have that before the law existed, surely you and I can have it after the law was fulfilled. The reason we can do it is because neither salvation nor spirituality is contingent upon keeping the law, but upon believing the Lord:

> 1 What then shall we say that Abraham our father has found according to the flesh? 2 For if Abraham was justified by works, he has something to boast about, but not before God. 3 For what does the Scripture say? "Abraham believed God, and it was accounted to him for righteousness." 4 Now to him who works, the wages are not counted as grace but as debt. 5 But to him who does not work but believes on Him who justifies the ungodly, his faith is accounted for righteousness, —Romans 4:1–5

Paul is pointing out that whether in the Old Testament or the New Testament, the means of salvation is the same: faith. Faith is nothing more or less than believing God. That's what Adam and Eve did not do; that's why they fell. Since the fall of man came about because of unbelief, the restoration of man is dependent upon belief. Abraham was not justified because he kept the Jewish law. That law didn't even exist in his day. Rather he was justified and declared righteous because he believed God. Believing God is not limited to the New Testament.

When I am teaching in any group of Christians, one of my favorite questions to ask is, "How were people saved in the Old Testament?" Almost invariably the answer is, "By the keeping of the law." But that is just not so. If it were, then no one in the Old Testament, including Abraham, could ever get saved, because no one could ever keep the law. And even if they could, it would not save them because Paul told us plainly that "by the works of the law shall no flesh be justified" (Galatians 2:16). "Well, then, by animal sacrifice." Yet Hebrews 10:4 tells us "it is not possible that the blood of bulls and of goats should take away sins." So then, how were the Old Testament saints saved? The same way the New Testament saints are saved: by grace through faith (Ephesians 2:8–9).

"Then what was the purpose of the animal sacrifices in the Old Testament? Why did those people have to continually make sacrifices to God?"

In Romans 10:17, Paul told us, "So then faith cometh by hearing, and hearing by the word of God." The Old Testament rituals were only a shadow of the true redeeming atonement that would take place when Jesus Christ, the Lamb of God, would shed His own blood for the remission of the sins of the people. By rehearsing that future event symbolically, day after day, in the tabernacle and temple using sacrificial animals to represent the true Lamb of God, the people actually saw, demonstrated continually, the atoning death of their Savior. With their eyes they "heard" over and over the Word of God, the message of grace, the gospel of the coming Messiah.

In the New Testament, after the resurrection of the Lord Jesus Christ, people are saved by grace through faith in the finished work of Christ on the cross. In the Old Testament, they were saved by grace through faith in the future work of Christ on the cross. However in both instances, the means of salvation is the same: by grace through faith. That's why Paul referred to Abraham as "the father of faith," "the father of all them that believe . . . Therefore it [salvation] is of faith, that it might be by grace; to the end the promise might be sure to all the seed; not to that only which is of the law, but to that also which is of the faith of Abraham; who is the father of us all" (Romans 4:11, 16).

Salvation comes by grace through faith. This faith comes from hearing. In the Old Testament, hearing came through the ritualistic sacrifices. Every time the people saw their sins placed upon the head of a scapegoat that was then cast out into the wilderness, they saw the picture of the coming Messiah, "the Lamb of God, which taketh away the sin of the world" (John 1:29). Every time they watched as an animal was slaughtered and its blood sprinkled upon the altar of the temple, they would say to themselves: "That animal speaks of the Messiah who will one day come to take my sin from me. It will be placed upon Him and He will be killed, shedding His blood for the remission of my sin. He will die spiritually that I might be born again spiritually."

Notice, I said the people in the Old Testament were saved; I didn't say they were born again. I use the term saved to indicate they were justified (counted righteous), but they were not born again because there was no provision for the new birth until after the resurrection of the Lord Jesus

Christ. They were counted righteous, but they did not become righteous until their spirits were re-created and the Holy Spirit came to live within them. That event did not occur until after the day of Pentecost. Athough they were not born again until after the coming of the Messiah, the Old Testament saints were saved the same way you and I are: by grace through faith. They were saved by believing God, by trusting in His promise of redemption through the shed blood of His own Son. Salvation has always been a gift of God's grace freely received by faith, not a reward attained by works of the law.

So Abraham was not saved by keeping the law. He was not saved by works. He wasn't saved by observing a set of dos and don'ts. He wasn't even saved by being circumcised.

"Yes, but Abraham was circumcised."

Yes, he was. But *when* was he circumcised?

> 8 Blessed is the man to whom the Lord shall not impute sin." 9 Does this blessedness then come upon the circumcised only, or upon the uncircumcised also? For we say that faith was accounted to Abraham for righteousness. 10 How then was it accounted? While he was circumcised, or uncircumcised? Not while circumcised, but while uncircumcised. 11 And he received the sign of circumcision, a seal of the righteousness of the faith which he had while still uncircumcised, that he might be the father of all those who believe, though they are uncircumcised, that righteousness might be imputed to them also, —Romans 4:8–11

Abraham was not saved by being circumcised, but rather circumcision was given as a sign he was saved, separated from the world and joined to God. It wasn't circumcision that saved Abraham; it was only a seal of the covenant between him and God. Circumcision didn't make the covenant; it only attested to it. It was faith that made the covenant a reality in Abraham's life.

Today, New Testament believers are not circumcised as a sign of our covenant of salvation. Rather we participants in the new covenant are baptized as a sign of our identification with Jesus Christ in His sacrificial death, burial, and resurrection. We identify with Christ in His death in the same way the Old Testament saints identified with the death of the coming Messiah; through faith.

II. The Sons of Abraham (7)

3:7 Therefore know that *only* those who are of faith are sons of Abraham.

Notice, they who are of faith, not of works or the law, these are the children of Abraham. There are two words in Greek translated either as children or sons in the *King James Version*. In this instance, the Greek word is *huios*, which would more correctly be translated as sons (as it is in most modern translations such as the *New American Standard Bible*). The other Greek word is *teknon*. We will consider the difference in these two words more closely when we study chapter 4, but in this particular verse Paul was saying, "Know then that those who are of faith, these are the sons of Abraham."

Now as we remember from Genesis, Abraham had two male children, one by his wife Sarah and the other by her handmaid Hagar. Out of Ishmael (the offspring of Abraham and Hagar) there came the race of people we call the Arabs. From Isaac (the offspring of Abraham and Sarah) there came the Hebrews. So Abraham produced two sets of offspring: the Arabs and the Jews.

Abraham also produced two other sets of offspring: a natural race called the Jews and a spiritual race called the seed of Christ, the church universal of today.

We can learn a great deal about this spiritual race by looking at the Jewish nation today. The Jew is a natural example of the spiritual hidden Church. Some people today hold the Jews up as an example of how God washes His hands of a people who are unfaithful to Him, but God has never abandoned or forsaken the Jewish nation. Even though they have been in apostasy for two thousand years, God still honors His covenant with them. People may break God's covenant, but He never does. One day that covenant will be fulfilled in every detail, just as God has prophesied through His servants. In the meantime, the covenant is in full effect. That's why there is still a nation called Israel to this day, and why there will continue to be one.

What does that have to do with us under the new covenant? A great deal. Recently I was reading a historical volume entitled *Cambridge Ancient History*. Although it was not a Christian publication, the author noted it was amazing to trace the rise and fall of nations in relation to how they treated Israel. He went on to give several examples of governments that had fallen as a result of their mistreatment of the Jews. Foremost in that category was the German Third Reich that Hitler boasted would last a thousand years. As we know, it did not last even twenty-five years. The reason is obvious. No government or nation which sets out to oppose and annihilate the people of the covenant can long endure.

Hilton Sutton, an authority in Bible prophecy, has often spoken about the Shah of Iran, calling attention to the fact that it was only two days after he turned his people against Israel that he was deposed from his throne and his regime began to crumble. God honors His Word.

That should be a source of great comfort and assurance to us today as participants in the new covenant. Even though we may fail, as the Jews have failed through the years, God will not fail. In His Word He has promised never to leave or forsake those who put their trust in Him. God keeps His promises. Once an individual or a group of individuals has entered into a covenant relationship with Him, that person or group becomes special to God. He will see to it that His part of that covenant agreement is kept. One of the provisions of that agreement is protection from those who would harm His covenant people.

It is important how we, as a people and a government, treat the nation of Israel. That also holds true in our relationship with other Christians — even those who are not in fellowship with the Lord at the moment. That doesn't matter: they are still God's covenant people. You do not oppose God's chosen ones without finding yourself in opposition to God — and that is not an enviable position to be in. Jesus warned us not to judge or condemn anyone. In so doing, we only call down cursing upon our own heads. Because of the law of sowing and reaping, what we wish upon others, especially those of the covenant, will come back upon us. We would do well to learn to love others, as we would be loved: "for this is the law and the prophets" (Matthew 7:12).

III. The True Israel

Notice in verse 7, sons come into being through faith. Then how do children come into being? What is the difference between the children of Abraham and the sons of Abraham? The children of Abraham are the physical Jews; the sons of Abraham are those who put their faith in Christ.

In Jesus' day, the Jews prided themselves on the fact they were the "seed of Abraham." But Jesus told them God could raise up physical seed from the stones of the earth (Matthew 3:9). The true seed of Abraham is spiritual. Becoming a seed (a son) of Abraham does not depend upon a person's

nationality or race, but upon his faith. Just because a person is a Jew physically does not mean he is one spiritually.

In Romans 9:1 through 8, Paul made this point very clear:

> 1 I tell the truth in Christ, I am not lying, my conscience also
> bearing me witness in the Holy Spirit, 2 that I have great sorrow
> and continual grief in my heart. 3 For I could wish that I myself
> were accursed from Christ for my brethren, my countrymen
> according to the flesh, 4 who are Israelites, to whom pertain
> the adoption, the glory, the covenants, the giving of the law, the
> service of God, and the promises; 5 of whom are the fathers and
> from whom, according to the flesh, Christ came, who is over all,
> the eternally blessed God. Amen. 6 But it is not that the word
> of God has taken no effect. For they are not all Israel who are
> of Israel, 7 nor are they all children because they are the seed
> of Abraham; but, "In Isaac your seed shall be called." 8 That is,
> those who are the children of the flesh, these are not the children
> of God; but the children of the promise are counted as the seed.

Not all those who are Israelites are sons of Abraham. Only those born of
the promise; that is, those born again by the Spirit of God through faith in
Jesus Christ.

Within the nation of Israel, there are *teknon* and there are *huios*. There
are the children of Abraham, and there are the true sons of Abraham. The
children were born Jewish, but one day those children exercised faith in
the Lord Jesus Christ and were changed from children to sons. In the same
way, you and I were born into this earth, but one day we exercised faith in
the Lord Jesus Christ and became sons of Abraham. We became the true
Israel.

Notice again Romans 9:7: "Neither, because they are the seed of Abraham,
are they all children: but, In Isaac shall thy seed be called." What does this
mean? Ishmael and Isaac were both the seed of Abraham, but Paul pointed out that just because they were Abraham's seed, it did not make them
both sons of Abraham. Only Isaac was called the son of Abraham. Why?
Wasn't Ishmael just as much a son of Abraham as Isaac? Why was Ishmael
rejected and Isaac accepted?

Some people say Ishmael was rejected because he was born out of wed-
lock by Hagar, a bondmaid. But that's not so. Natural birth matters nothing

to God. It is not the legitimacy of a person's birth that makes him acceptable to God; rather, it is his faith that makes him approved of the Lord.
Take the example of Esau and Jacob. Both were legitimate sons of Isaac,
twins born of the same mother, Rebecca. Yet even though Jacob was a
cheat and a scoundrel, he received the blessing of God, whereas Esau, the
firstborn and rightful heir, was rejected of God. This doesn't make sense in
the natural. Esau may have been a better person than Jacob. Why was he
rejected and his conniving brother accepted? Paul explains:

> 9 For this is the word of promise: "At this time I will come and
> Sarah shall have a son." 10 And not only this, but when Rebecca
> also had conceived by one man, even by our father Isaac 11 (for
> the children not yet being born, nor having done any good or
> evil, that the purpose of God according to election might stand,
> not of works but of Him who calls), 12 it was said to her, "The
> older shall serve the younger." 13 As it is written, "Jacob I have
> loved, but Esau I have hated." —Romans 9:9–13

In this passage Paul made it clear that God chose Jacob over Esau while
they were still in the womb. Before they were even born, before they had
done anything either good or bad, the Lord accepted Jacob and rejected
Esau. Why? He looked ahead at their lives and saw the faith of Jacob and
the unbelief of Esau. He made His choice based on His foreknowledge of
their faith. Because He knew Jacob would believe Him in the future and
Esau would not, God made His choice between them. Not according to
their actions in the natural realm, but in accordance to their faith. Not of
works, good or bad, but by faith in God.

Paul used this point to prove natural birth does not make a person acceptable to God. Jacob went on to become Israel. He produced twelve
sons who were born of two different wives and two handmaids (Genesis
35:23–26). Yet all those sons were men of faith, so they became the heads
of the twelve tribes of Israel. Natural birth, whether legitimate or illegitimate, is not the determining factor in a person's election by God. It is faith.

The genealogy of our Lord Jesus Christ is given in both Matthew 1 and
Luke 3. Sprinkled throughout His natural family, we find several Gentiles.
Three of the four women mentioned in Matthew's version were Gentiles:
Rahab, Ruth, and Bathsheba. Even Jesus was not a pure Jew by birth. He
was a son of Abraham not because of His physical descent from Abraham
but because He was born of the Holy Spirit of God. It is not natural birth

but spiritual birth that makes a person a son of Abraham and therefore a child of God.

In Romans 9:7 when Paul said, "Neither, because they are the seed of Abraham, are they all children: but, in Isaac shall thy seed be called," he was saying Isaac represents faith, and it is the seed of faith that counts with God. This word "seed" is singular. We will be encountering this word throughout chapter 3 of Galatians.

"(For the children being not yet born, neither having done any good or evil, that the purpose of God according to election might stand, not of works, but of him that calleth;) it was said unto her, The elder shall serve the younger" (Romans 9:11–12). Do you remember what Paul said about his call in Galatians 1? He said God chose him by grace from his mother's womb. It has to be grace to choose from the womb because the person has not yet had an opportunity to do anything to merit being chosen by God. Election (redemption, righteousness) cannot be by works. It is entirely God's doing without regard to our actions, either good or bad.

"As it is written, Jacob have I loved, but Esau have I hated" (Romans 9:13). This is a quote by Paul of Malachi 1:2–3. Some people have difficulty with that. They think God is unfair because He judges people before they are even born. However, God is not unfair. His opinion of a person is not determined by that person's actions; it is determined by the amount of faith God sees on the inside of them.

Since He can see the end from the beginning, the Lord doesn't have to wait until an individual has lived out his full life span before He knows what he or she has on the inside. The presence or absence of faith is evident to our heavenly Father from the time of our conception.

God's election or choice before birth is not unfair; it's simply based on foreknowledge. A person's fate is not predetermined or predestined so he or she has no choice in the matter. The apostle Peter addressed his first epistle to the "elect according to the foreknowledge of God the Father" (1 Peter 1:2). God's election is from before the time of birth, but that election is based on His foreknowledge of the person's life, not what that individual will do, but the amount of faith he or she will demonstrate.

Election (salvation) is by grace based upon faith; it is not a product of works. If election is not of works, then neither is righteousness because no one can keep by works of the law what he never earned by works of the law. We who are saved by grace through faith "are kept by the power of God through faith unto salvation" (1 Peter 1:5).

Righteousness, like redemption, is all by grace through faith.

IV. The First Jew (8)

3:8 And the Scripture, foreseeing that God would justify the Gentiles by faith, preached the gospel to Abraham beforehand, saying, "In you all the nations shall be blessed."

. . . In thee shall all nations be blessed.

This is a quote from Genesis 12:3 in which God promised Abraham that because he believed Him, he would be blessed and that through him all nations would be blessed. "All nations" refers not only to the Gentiles, the non-Jews, but also to the Jews, because as yet the Jewish nation did not exist.

And the scripture, foreseeing that God would justify the heathen through faith . . .

Who are the heathen? You and I. We non-Jews are referred to as Gentiles or heathen, in the natural. How are we saved? Through faith. If that is so, how are Jews saved? The same way, through faith. At the time God gave this promise to Abraham there were no Jews; everyone was a Gentile, a heathen, even Abraham. As Paul says of Abraham in Romans :

10 How then was it accounted? While he was circumcised, or uncircumcised? Not while circumcised, but while uncircumcised. . . . 13 For the promise that he would be the heir of the world was not to Abraham or to his seed through the law, but through the righteousness of faith. . . . 19 And not being weak in faith, he did not consider his own body, already dead (since he was about a hundred years old), and the deadness of Sarah's womb. 20 He did not waver at the promise of God through unbelief, but was strengthened in faith, giving glory to God, 21 and being fully convinced that what He had promised He was also able to perform. 22 And therefore "it was accounted to him for righteousness." —Romans 4:10, 13, 19–22

Abraham was not yet a physical Jew when he was justified. He was saved by faith, just as any other person. Abraham was the first Jew. He was not born a Jew, nor did he become one by circumcision of the flesh. Instead he was circumcised after he believed as a sign of his covenant relationship with God. The first Jew, then, was a heathen who one day exercised faith in God and from that day forth was acceptable to God by his faith. In Abraham, the man of faith, God began a new supernatural race of beings called Jews. If Abraham, the first Jew, was saved by grace through faith and not by works, then his descendants are saved the same way. There is no distinction then between Jews and Gentiles. All are saved the same way, by faith in the finished work of the Lord Jesus Christ.

. . . Preached before the gospel unto Abraham, saying, In thee shall all nations be blessed."

Abraham received the Word of the Lord while still a heathen. His belief in that Word changed him from a heathen into a believer. Abraham became the first Jew because of his faith. The mark or sign of Abraham's faith was circumcision. The covenant was established on faith, not works. Circumcision was only the corresponding action of faith in God's promise of salvation by grace. Circumcision did not save Abraham; it was only an outward sign that he had truly been set aside by God and had received salvation.

Who preached the gospel to Abraham so he could believe and be saved? We find the answer in Genesis 12 where the Lord appeared to Abraham while he was still living in Ur of Chaldees. Jesus Christ preached the gospel to Abraham (v. 17). The word *Chalde* comes from an ancient Armenian word meaning moon worship. The Chaldeans were heathens, moon worshippers. Abraham was likely no different from the other pagans of his day and nation. However, seeing his faith, God chose Abraham from that heathenistic society and appeared to him to preach (declare) to him the gospel.

What was the gospel Abraham received of the Lord? What does the word *gospel* mean? Good news. What good news gets a person saved? The message, "God so loved the world, that he gave his only begotten Son, that whosoever believeth in him should not perish, but have everlasting life" (John 3:16).

People are saved by the good news that the Son of God came to this earth to die for the sins of man, He was dead and buried, and He arose from the grave on the third day to ascend into heaven. He will one day return to receive all those who have put their faith and trust in Him. Isn't that basically what we tell people to confess in order to be saved? Don't we teach them "that if thou shalt confess with thy mouth the Lord Jesus, and shalt believe in thine heart that God hath raised him from the dead, thou shalt be saved" (Romans 10:9)?

In order for a person to be saved, he must hear the Good News. He cannot believe what he hasn't heard. That's what Paul was emphasizing eight verses later when he said "faith cometh by hearing, and hearing by the word of God" (Romans 10:17). If Abraham had to believe God to be saved, he had to first hear from God, because he couldn't very well believe what he had never heard. In order for Abraham to be saved, he had to hear the gospel. The only person preaching the gospel in Abraham's day was the Lord Himself. That's the reason He appeared to Abraham in Ur of the Chaldees — to declare to him the good news. Abraham believed God, he accepted and acted upon the Word of God, and so he was declared righteous. Abraham was saved by the grace of God through faith in His Son.

What proof do we have of this fact? In John 8:56 the Lord Jesus Christ said to the Pharisees: "Your father Abraham rejoiced to see my day: and he saw it, and was glad." Abraham saw the day of Jesus Christ. He was saved by looking forward to the future work of the Savior, just as you and I were saved by looking backward upon that finished work at Calvary.

How was Abraham, the first Jew, saved? By believing the gospel of the death, burial, and resurrection of the coming Messiah. How did he receive this gospel? It was proclaimed to him by the Lord Himself. How then were the rest of the Jews saved in Old Testament days? By believing the gospel. How was it preached to them? By the Lord Himself through the ritualistic sacrifices of the temple worship that portrayed before their eyes continually the sacrificial, atoning work of the future Messiah.

When Jesus told the Pharisees Abraham rejoiced to see the coming of His day, they were incensed:

> 57 Then the Jews said to Him, "You are not yet fifty years old, and have You seen Abraham?" 58 Jesus said to them, "Most assuredly, I say to you, before Abraham was, I AM." 59 Then they took up stones to throw at Him; but Jesus hid Himself and went out of the temple, going through the midst of them, and so passed by. —John 8:57–59

Why did the Jews try to stone Jesus? They were angry because He dared to claim He was God, the All-Knowing One, the All-Sufficient One, the Ever-Existent One, the Great I Am. They didn't see who He really was. They looked at the outward man, but they didn't perceive the Spirit within Him.

Abraham recognized the Lord and believed on Him whose day he saw coming. His belief saved him, not his works.

V. Blessed with Abraham (9–10)

3:9 So then those who *are* of faith are blessed with believing Abraham.

They which be of faith are blessed . . .

Note, this does not say "those which be of works are blessed" but "those which be of faith."

. . . with believing Abraham.

Believing is faith in action. It is taking the faith on the inside and putting it into action on the outside.

If you are a Christian but are not being blessed along with believing Abraham, you may be wondering what's wrong. Why are others around you being blessed continually while you go through life just getting by, never really enjoying life in all its abundance? The answer is probably because you are not taking the faith residing within you and putting it to work for the cause of Christ and of His kingdom.

Abraham wasn't content with just sitting and confessing his faith. He put faith into action. Faith is a little like a muscle. We all have muscles, but some of us have much larger and more powerful muscles than others. Why? Those with strong muscles are usually those who continually use the muscles they have. In the same way, people are blessed not by having faith but by exercising faith.

It is not hearing the Word alone that matters, though we must hear it. It's doing the Word we hear and believing that actually produces results. It's the doing of faith that brings the blessing of Abraham.

3:10 ¶ For as many as are of the works of the law are under the curse; for it is written, "*Cursed is everyone who does not continue in all things which are written in the book of the law, to do them.*"

This is a quote from Deuteronomy 27:26: "Cursed be he that confirmeth not all the words of this law to do them." What Paul is saying here is the curse of the law existed before the law was given. What is the threefold curse of the law pronounced upon anyone who does not keep it in every detail? Poverty, sickness, and death. Didn't each of these things exist before the law was ever given to man? If these things existed before the law was given, and if they still exist today after the law has been given, then the law does not remove the curse. The curse is still there and will be until the end of the age when it will be totally annihilated and removed forever. Until such time, you and I can live free of the curse only one way, by being in Christ Jesus who took the curse upon Himself for us at Calvary and by walking in the Spirit so we do not fulfill the lusts of the flesh.

As believers, we are not subject to the curse because we are redeemed from it. We were crucified with Christ, nevertheless we live; yet not us, but Christ lives in us. And the life we now live in the flesh we live by the faith of the Son of God, who loved us, and gave Himself for us (Galatians 2:20). Our new life is marked by the blessing of Abraham that comes upon us as we exercise faith to receive it. Because of what God has done for us in Christ Jesus, we who are of faith are truly blessed with faithful Abraham.

3:11–20 The Abrahamic Covenant

I. The Law Is Not of Faith (11–12)

In our last chapter, we looked at verse 10, which stated that those who are subject to the law are under a curse, because "cursed is every one that continueth not in all things which are written in the book of the law to do them." We noted no one is able to keep every point of the entire law; therefore, we all come under the curse of the law. The law not only makes us slaves to a system of dos and don'ts, it actually condemns us because we are not able to live up to that system. The law thus becomes our condemnation rather than our deliverance. That's why we stated the law was never given by God as a means of salvation but only to cause man to realize his inability to save himself. He can then turn to God to receive the free gift of salvation bought and paid for by the shed blood of His Son Jesus Christ.

Once salvation has been received by grace through faith, we believers sometimes make the mistake of trying to please God by works of righteousness: We read our Bible, pray, fast, witness to others about Christ, attend church regularly, pay our tithes, give offerings, do good works, and on and on. All this is good. The mistake we make in doing all these things is thinking by doing them we are attaining or retaining righteousness because we are pleasing God. The truth is, the Word of God has made it clear it is faith that pleases God, not works of the law. If it was not works that saved us, it naturally follows it is not works that make us spiritual. On the contrary, many times our works, our own self-efforts, prevent us from fulfilling righteousness because they get our eyes off the source of our righteousness and focus them on ourselves.

3:11 But that no one is justified by the law in the sight of God *is* evident, for *"the just shall live by faith."*

Continuing with this same idea in verse 11, Paul points out no one is justified (made righteous) by the law, but by faith. We are saved by faith to live a life of faith. To begin our Christian life by faith and then attempt to live it by works is to fall back into legalism. A person cannot remain righteous by works any more than he can become righteous by works. The Christian life is one of faith from beginning to end. The Bible tells us "the just [those who are saved by faith] shall live by faith."

Why then do we work? Not to gain the Lord's favor. He was pleased with us before He saved us. That's what grace is: God's favor. It was by His favor we were saved in the first place. Therefore, we cannot retain His favor by works any more than we received His favor by working for it.

No, we work for God because we love Him and are grateful for His wonderful works. We don't work to please God; rather our works are evidence that He is already pleased with us!

In verse 11, the twofold theme of the book of Galatians is brought out again: 1) Justification by faith and 2) Spirituality by faith.

Works do not justify a person in the sight of God. They may justify him in the sight of men, but not in God's eyes.

"But didn't James say that Abraham was justified by works?"

Yes, he did, in James 2:21: "Was not Abraham our father justified by works, when he had offered Isaac his son upon the altar?" That action was a work, but Abraham's work did not justify him before God; it justified him before men. You see, men needed to know Abraham believed and God accounted that belief unto him as righteousness. The same is true in our lives. People need to see our good works and glorify our Father in heaven, just as Jesus said in Matthew 5:16. But Jesus did not say we were saved by those good works.

"Then if we are not saved by good works, what is their purpose?"

The purpose of works is not our salvation; it's the salvation of others! What do I mean by that? Simply this: The world cannot see on the inside of us. To them we are simply human beings like them. By our outward appearances, we may seem to be; but God looks at the heart. He sees the faith in our heart and that faith pleases Him. We don't need to prove our faith to God for Him to save us, but other people need to see some outward manifestation of our faith if they are to be convinced we have something they don't have. The world can't see our faith; it can see only the results of our faith, our good works.

Works, then, like tongues, are not a sign for the believer but for the unbeliever (1 Corinthians 14:22). Our good works are not the means by which we win points with God; they are the means by which we win souls for God. Do you think God is more interested in our winning points or in our being like Jesus of Nazareth? Which of these two do you think is more pleasing to God? Which of the two do you think will have the most positive effect on unbelievers? Don't you think He's more interested in our being anointed by the Holy Spirit with power and going about doing good, healing all who are oppressed of the devil, because God is with us (Acts 10:38)?

. . . The just shall live by faith.

This is a quote from Habakkuk 2:4: "The just shall live by his faith." Are you just? If so, how did you become just? By faith. How do you live now that you are just? By faith. Faith gets a person into the kingdom of God, and faith keeps him going once he's in. We don't start by faith and then turn to the law any more than we start with the law and stay with the law. No, we started by faith, and we will stay with faith. We who are just live by our faith.

3:12 Yet the law is not of faith, but *"the man who does them shall live by them."*

This verse is a quote from Leviticus 18:5, part of the law given by God through Moses to the children of Israel: "Ye shall therefore keep my statutes, and my judgments: which if a man do, he shall live in them." If we shrug off faith and true spirituality and try to attain righteousness by our self-efforts, then we are obliged to live our whole lives by the law. Once we abide by the law, we are obligated to abide in the law. Deuteronomy 28 warns that anyone who does not continue in the law brings the curse of the law upon himself. It's not easy to continue in the law, because to violate one part of it is to violate it all.

When non-Jews refer to the law, we usually associate it with the Ten Commandments, but that wasn't the whole of the Jewish law. The Law is the entire first five books of the Bible. There are over 615 separate commandments contained in those five books. To keep 614 of these commandments is not enough — to offend in one is to offend in all. Anyone who thinks he can attain righteousness by keeping the law has his work cut out for him!

It is impossible to keep every part of the law. This is one reason the Bible teaches no flesh is justified by works of the law (Galatians 2:16). No flesh is perfect enough to keep the law a whole lifetime. To break the law is to call down the curse upon the offender. That curse still exists, is still active, still operative. That's why Christians can't live any way they want and still prosper in every facet of their lives.

It's true we are no longer under the old covenant, the law. We're under the new covenant, but that does not mean we are lawless. Our Lord removed us from the curse of the law, so the blessing of Abraham could come upon us. However, if we remove ourselves from His circle of protection by consciously committing sin, then the effects if the curse can still come upon us (unless that sin is removed).

"Well, if no one could keep the law, how in the world did the people in the Old Testament become justified? What happened when they kept breaking the law over and over?"

They kept offering blood sacrifices over and over. Those sacrifices didn't save them; they just pointed to the one who could save them — the coming Messiah. Animal sacrifices were simply a means of teaching the people about the future Christ who would one day come to offer Himself as the Lamb of God to take away the sin of the world permanently. The blood shed on the Old Testament altars was a type of the atoning blood of Jesus Christ, which alone has the power to wash away sin and cleanse unrighteousness.

The Old Testament saints were cleansed of sin the same way you and I are, by the shedding of blood: "without shedding of blood is no remission" (Hebrews 9:22). The difference is the blood of animals could never take away sins; it could only cover them up until the blood of the Lamb would remove those sins forever. You and I no longer have to continually offer the blood of animals for forgiveness of sin; we simply apply the blood of Christ to our sins. How do we do that? The answer is found in 1 John 1:9: "If we confess our sins, he is faithful and just to forgive us our sins, and to cleanse us from all unrighteousness."

If the blood of Christ cleansed us from our sin so we could be made acceptable to God in the first place, then it is that same blood that continues to cleanse us from all unrighteousness today. If it made us clean, it keeps us clean. The way to fulfill all righteousness and walk in divine protection is not by keeping the law but by walking in constant fellowship with the Lord Jesus Christ.

II. The Great Exchange (13–14)

A. Christ Becomes the Curse

> **3:13 ¶ Christ has redeemed us from the curse of the law, having become a curse for us (for it is written, *"Cursed is everyone who hangs on a tree"*),**

The Greek tense used in this sentence indicates this is a settled action. Christ has — once and for all — redeemed us from the curse of the law.

. . . Being made a curse for us . . .

The way our Lord redeemed us from the curse was to become the curse. What does it mean, He became the curse? Since He was absolute righteousness, He had to actually become sin. Since He was God's health, He had to become sickness. Since He had the riches of heaven, He had to lay those riches aside and become poverty. Why did He do all that? For us.

In 2 Corinthians 8:9, Paul told us "For ye know the grace of our Lord Jesus Christ, that, though he was rich, yet for your sakes he became poor, that ye through his poverty might be rich." In order for us to become what Christ is, He had to become what we were. He became accursed that we might become blessed. He became sick that we might become healthy. He became poor that we might become rich. These are the three categories of the curse of the law: poverty, sickness, and spiritual death. In each of these cases, Jesus Christ became the curse that we might be set free from the curse.

B. The Curse Brings Death

Let's consider the case of spiritual death. Did Jesus die spiritually for us? Look at 2 Corinthians 5:21: "For he [God] hath made him [Christ] to be sin for us, who knew no sin; that we might be made the righteousness of God in him." The one who knew no sin became sin for us, that we might be made the righteousness of God in Him. We were unrighteous; Jesus Christ was righteous. God made His own son unrighteous, so you and I could be made righteous. Christ took our unrighteousness, and we took His righteousness. What an exchange!

Our Lord took upon Himself our sinful human nature so we might receive His righteous, divine nature. He took our sin in exchange for His holiness. If that is so, if by receiving Him we received His nature and holiness, why then would we ever try to achieve a holiness of our own? Could we ever hope to attain by our weak, human efforts what God poured out upon us freely through the person of His own dear Son? Who would be so foolish as to try and attain a righteousness of his own when he has already freely received the divine righteousness of the very Son of God? Can you see why Paul called these Galatians foolish?

That exchange sounds so good some people have a hard time believing it. That's why they have a hard time receiving it — because that is precisely the way it is received, by belief. That belief is called faith. The righteousness of God in Christ is received as you would receive any free gift, "For by grace are ye saved through faith; and that not of yourselves: it is the gift of God: not of works, lest any man should boast" (Ephesians 2:8–9). The same Paul who wrote these words also wrote in Romans 5:17 that righteousness is a gift. What did we have to give our Lord in exchange for His righteousness? Nothing. Absolutely nothing. If we'd had to give anything to receive it, then it would not have been a free gift.

There was an exchange. Christ gave us something, and He took something in return, but what Christ took from us was not anything we wanted. He took our sin, sickness, and poverty from us and gave us His righteousness, health, and riches.

"Where does it say that Christ took our sickness?" In Isaiah 53:4 and 5: "Surely he hath borne our griefs, and carried our sorrows: yet we did esteem him stricken, smitten of God, and afflicted. But he was wounded for our transgressions, he was bruised for our iniquities: the chastisement of our peace was upon him; and with his stripes we are healed."

Matthew wrote, "When the even was come, they brought unto him many that were possessed with devils: and he cast out the spirits with his word, and healed all that were sick: that it might be fulfilled which was spoken by Esaias the prophet, saying, Himself took our infirmities, and bare our sicknesses" (Matthew 8:16–17).

Peter wrote, "Who his own self bare our sins in his own body on the tree, that we, being dead to sins, should live unto righteousness: by whose stripes ye were healed" (1 Peter 2:24).

Jesus became the curse of sickness for us, that we might be made well. Was Jesus ever sick? There is no record that He was. He never knew a day of sickness in His life. He certainly didn't bring any sickness with Him from heaven; there was none there to bring. He proclaimed He came to this earth to do the will of His Father in heaven. While He was here, He went about doing good and healing all those who were oppressed of the devil (Acts 10:38). But when Jesus Christ went to the cross of Calvary, there He took upon Himself our sickness, just as He took upon Himself our sins, so we might receive His wholeness as well as His holiness. He also took our poverty, so we might receive His riches. Jesus became our poverty on the cross. He was prosperous when He walked on the earth just as He was sinless and whole in body and mind.

Where did Jesus become sin? On the cross. When did He become sickness? And poverty? Ot the cross. Why? Jesus became these things ot the cross because it is written, "Cursed is every one that hangeth on a tree" (not everyone that walketh on the earth). Therefore, if Christ became a curse for us that we might become blessed, if He took upon Himself our sin, sickness, poverty, and spiritual death, that we might receive His righteousness, health, riches, and eternal and abundant life, then why would we ever strive to get these things for ourselves? All we need to do, all we *can* do, is receive them freely as a gift from God the Father who laid our sins on His own son and nailed them to a tree. That means if Jesus walked a life free from sin on this earth, so can you and I. If He walked free from sickness and disease, so can we. If He lived free from poverty, we can too.

"But Jesus said He had no place to lay His head."

That's right. That's because He was a minister. It does not mean He was poor, only that He was itinerant. Jesus traveled with a company of twelve disciples, plus many others who accompanied Him wherever He went. Yet we have no record they ever went hungry or naked or without shelter because of a lack of provision. Even when He sent out the seventy and commanded them explicitly not to take anything with them, not even a change of clothes, when they came back He later asked them: " 'When I sent you without purse, and scrip, and shoes, lacked ye any thing?' And they said 'Nothing'" (Luke 22:35). Jesus was never without means. He had a moneybag carried by Judas Iscariot. It must have been amply filled because we know Judas embezzled from it. Jesus gave to the poor, and poor people don't give to poor people. He wore nice clothes that were gambled over by the soldiers who crucified Him. Jesus was not poor. Not until He went to the cross. There He became poor that we might be made rich.

Although artists and sculptors always represent Jesus on the cross wearing a loincloth, that is not historically accurate. When the Romans crucified a person, he was always completely naked. That was part of the shame of the cross, which we sing about in many of our old hymns of faith. On Calvary, Jesus Christ, the Son of God, was not only stripped of His vestments, he was stripped of His position, dignity, holiness, righteousness, riches, health — even His very fellowship with His Father in heaven: "My God, my God, why hast thou forsaken me?" (Matthew 27:46). He was rejected by men and rejected by God. He became sin, He became sickness, and He became poverty for you and me.

Aren't you glad Jesus Christ took the curse, so we might receive the blessing? He did that once and for all. When Christ rose from the grave, He did not arise sinful, sick, or poor. Our Lord is no longer sin, sickness, or poverty because He is no longer dead! He is alive and well and living in glory where all the riches of heaven belong to Him. "As he is, so are we in this world" (1 John 4:17). That means we are also alive and well and living in His glory, beneficiaries of all that is His.

C. The Blessing of Abraham

3:14 that the blessing of Abraham might come upon the Gentiles in Christ Jesus, that we might receive the promise of the Spirit through faith.

Notice it is the curse of the law (v. 13), but the blessing of Abraham. That's very interesting. If Christ redeemed us from the curse that we might receive the blessing, why didn't Paul say we have been redeemed from the curse of the law that the blessing of the law might come on us? Why did he switch from the curse of the law to the blessing of Abraham? It is because the two are the same. The same blessing you and I received by receiving the Lord Jesus Christ into our lives is the same blessing we would have received had we been able to keep the law to absolute perfection. Since Jesus perfectly fulfilled the law for us, we receive the blessing as though we ourselves had qualified for it. This blessing is the same blessing Abraham received, not because he kept the law to perfection — there was no law for him to keep — but because he believed God. Therefore, it is possible to walk in the blessing of the law and not even know the law.

The law was added 430 years after Abraham lived on this earth. Abraham was born, lived out his lifetime, and died before the law was ever even given. Yet he walked in blessing. Here you and I are today these thousands of years after the law was given and fulfilled, yet we receive the same blessing as Abraham. If Abraham walked free of the law, so can you and I. Paul was trying to instruct the people in Galatia: Never let anyone put you under a law that you, like Abraham, were never subject to in the first place.

"Through Jesus Christ; that we might receive the promise of the Spirit through faith" (v. 14). Notice also it is through Jesus, not through the law, we are made able to receive the promise of the Spirit. By what means? Through faith. Again, it is not through the law we receive the blessing of Abraham; we receive it the same way Abraham received it, through faith.

III. The Abrahamic Covenant and Us (15–16)

3:15 ¶ Brethren, I speak in the manner of men: Though *it is* only a man's covenant, yet *if it is* confirmed, no one annuls or adds to it.

Here Paul begins an analogy between the Abrahamic covenant and a legal agreement. In order to make his point clear, he brings the covenant God made with Abraham into to human terms, likening it to a covenant (contract) drawn up between two individuals on earth.

. . . Yet if it be confirmed, no man disannulleth, or addeth thereto.

Once a contract between two people is drawn up, agreed upon, and confirmed (ratified) by their signatures, from that moment on the agreement is unalterable by either of the two parties without the consent of both parties.

Let's follow Paul's logic and apply this rule to the Abrahamic covenant. This contract between God and Abraham was drawn up and ratified before the law was ever given. The law was given to Moses, but the covenant was made between God and Abraham long before Moses was ever born. Therefore, Mosaic law could not supersede a previously existing contract, the Abrahamic covenant. If God were to break His agreement with Abraham after his death, He would be worse than a contract-breaker; He would be a cheater, because He would have waited until Abraham was dead to change His contract with him. That would make God lower than the level of men.

3:16 Now to Abraham and his Seed were the promises made. He does not say, "And to seeds," as of many, but as of one, "And to your Seed," who is Christ.

As we know, it takes two to make a contract. The two parties to the Abrahamic contract were God (first party who made the promises of blessing) and Abraham and his seed (second party to whom the promises of blessing were made).

. . . He saith not, And to seeds, as of many; but as of one, And to thy seed, which is Christ."

Who is the seed of Abraham who shared in his promised blessing? Jesus Christ. However, Christ didn't have any need of this contract. The contract releases us from poverty, sickness, and death. Christ had no need of release from these things because He was never subject to them. As the righteousness of God, He was not subject to unrighteousness. As the embodiment of divine health, He was not subject to sickness. As the creator of all riches, He was not subject to poverty. As the author of life, He was not subject to death. As the Son of God, He was not subject to any of these things — until that day when He became sin, until the time He took upon Himself our sickness, poverty, and death, so we might receive His righteousness, health, riches, and life:

> 7 who, in the days of His flesh, when He had offered up prayers and supplications, with vehement cries and tears to Him who was able to save Him from death, and was heard because of His godly fear, 8 though He was a Son, yet He learned obedience by the things which He suffered. 9 And having been perfected, He became the author of eternal salvation to all who obey Him,
> —Hebrews 5:7–9

As we have said, Christ took our nature as sinners. He took our place on the cross and suffered the chastisement of our sin that we might be made able to take His place as the righteousness of God. He became sin that we might become sons. The promises of God were made to Abraham's seed because God knew it was through the obedience of that seed that Abraham and all succeeding generations would be made righteous. The only way Abraham could be declared righteous was because there was coming a Messiah from his own offspring who would fulfill all righteousness for him.

The only way you and I can be declared righteous by God through faith is because we identify with Jesus Christ (the Seed of Abraham) who suffered our penalty and freed us from the law of sin and death. Without the Seed of Abraham, the Abrahamic covenant could never redeem anyone. It was through the Seed that the redemption would come.

It is in the Seed of Abraham you and I are included in the Abrahamic covenant. In Ephesians 1:3–12, Paul dealt with this subject of our identity with Christ the Redeemer, the Seed of Abraham:

> 3 Blessed be the God and Father of our Lord Jesus Christ, who has blessed us with every spiritual blessing in the heavenly places in Christ, 4 just as He chose us in Him before the foundation of the world, that we should be holy and without blame before Him in love, 5 having predestined us to adoption as sons by Jesus Christ to Himself, according to the good pleasure of His will, 6 to the praise of the glory of His grace, by which He made us accepted in the Beloved. 7 In Him we have redemption through

His blood, the forgiveness of sins, according to the riches of His grace 8 which He made to abound toward us in all wisdom and prudence, 9 having made known to us the mystery of His will, according to His good pleasure which He purposed in Himself, 10 that in the dispensation of the fullness of the times He might gather together in one all things in Christ, both which are in heaven and which are on earth—in Him. 11 In Him also we have obtained an inheritance, being predestined according to the purpose of Him who works all things according to the counsel of His will, 12 that we who first trusted in Christ should be to the praise of His glory.

According to verse 3, God "hath blessed us with all spiritual blessings in heavenly places in Christ." This is past tense. We have already been blessed.

"According as he hath chosen us in him before the foundation of the world" (v. 4). This word "chosen" in Greek means to call or speak out. You and I were called out by God. When? Before the foundation of the world.

"Having predestinated us unto the adoption of children by Jesus Christ to himself" (v. 5). According to verse 3, we were blessed of God before the foundation of the world. According to verse 4, we were chosen by God in Christ before the foundation of the world. Now in verse 5, we find we were predestined to become the children of God before the foundation of the world.

"Wherein he hath made us accepted in the beloved" (v. 6). When were we accepted in the beloved (that is, in Christ)? Before the foundation of the world.

In verse 7, we see that we have redemption. In verse 8, we read God has abounded toward us in all wisdom and prudence. In verse 9, we are told He has made known unto us the mystery of His will. In verse 11, we discover that we have obtained an inheritance. Finally in verses 11 and 12, we learn all this was planned and executed by God in accordance to His own will so that we who first trusted in Christ would become the praise of His glory.

However, as in the case of Abraham, how could God do all that for you and me before the foundation of the world? We weren't even there. How could God have blessed us along with faithful Abraham when neither we nor Abraham would even be born for billions upon billions of years? The only way God could pour out all those spiritual blessings upon us before the foundation of the world was through a representative who was there; His name is Jesus Christ.

Notice, every one of these statements is qualified. God "hath blessed us." Where? "In Christ" (v. 3). "He hath chosen" us. Where? "In him" (v. 4). God has "predestinated us unto the adoption of children." How? By "Jesus Christ" (v. 5). Who was called out before the foundation of the world? Jesus Christ. But He sat in the presence of God for you and me.

Christ didn't need to be called out. He didn't need to be chosen. He didn't need any of those things; He already had them. He did all this for us. He was our elected representative. He was not elected by us to represent us, rather He was elected (appointed) by God to stand in for us, to be our substitute in the heavenly courts, just as one day He would stand in for us as our substitute on the cross of Calvary. There He paid our penalty for us. Christ's death on the cross was our death. His burial was our burial. His resurrection and ascension into heaven to sit at the right hand of God the Father was our resurrection and ascension and coronation! His victory was our victory!

In Christ Jesus, you and I were called out before the foundation of the world. Before the earth was ever formed, our names were mentioned in the throne room of heaven. That's how personal our relationship to our heavenly Father is. He named us personally. He also named us personally when He made a covenant with Abraham.

"Now to Abraham and his seed were the promises made" (v. 16). You won't find your name or mine mentioned specifically anywhere in the Genesis accounts of the Abrahamic covenant. Nor will you find them specifically mentioned here in Paul's discussion of the covenant in the sixteenth verse of Galatians 3. But you will find that the covenant was made between God (first party) and Abraham and his seed (second party). It is in that phrase "and his seed," you and I are included in the covenant.

As the seed, Jesus was representing us. "If ye be Christ's, then are ye Abraham's seed, and heirs according to the promise" (3:29). The Abrahamic covenant was actually drawn up between God and us. The Abrahamic covenant actually reads like this: "Now to Abraham and Bob Yandian were the promises made." If you are a Christian, then you can substitute your own name for mine in that paraphrase of Galatians 3:16: "Now to Abraham and _____ were the promises made."

"He saith not, And to seeds, as of many; but as of one, And to thy seed, which is Christ" (v. 16). This is not a physical contract with a physical nation but a spiritual contract with a spiritual nation, that nation of which you and I are a part, the nation of His beloved.

"Seeds" are the Jews. "Seed" is the Lord Jesus Christ and all those who believe in Him. The Jews in Jesus' day thought they were the seed of Abraham because of their nationality, but the "seed" of Abraham was to bless "all nations." Abraham produced two offspring: a physical nation called Israel, and a spiritual race called the "seed." The covenant was for the spiritual race.

The promises of that contract were made to us individually through our representative, the Lord Jesus Christ. Our part of the covenant agreement was also fulfilled by our representative, by His life of perfect obedience to the Father in heaven and by His substitutionary death on the cross of Calvary. Now all of us who are in Christ Jesus are entitled to the blessing of Abraham.

IV. The Law and the Covenant (17–20)

3:17 And this I say, *that* the law, which was four hundred and thirty years later, cannot annul the covenant that was confirmed before by God in Christ, that it should make the promise of no effect.

Once the covenant agreement between Abraham and the Lord was confirmed, it could not be changed by one party without the consent of the other. This verse actually tells us it was the Lord Jesus who appeared to Abraham and received the covenant from God the Father.

If God had given the Jewish law to replace or supersede the Abrahamic covenant, He would have been guilty of breach of contract. If two parties agree to a contract that is to last forever, and then one of them changes the contract after the death of the other, the agreement has been broken. God could not change the terms of His covenant with Abraham 430 years after the death of Abraham without being guilty of breach of contract.

Did Abraham ever break his part of the contract? Yes, several times. For example, in Genesis we read he took Hagar, his wife's bondslave, and had a child by her. This was a breach of God's commandments upon which the covenant between Abraham and Him was made. Abraham also lied about his wife's relationship to him, saying she was his sister. Lying also constituted a breach of contract. Yet in spite of these and other offenses by Abraham, the covenant agreement was not disannulled.

God set that agreement into motion, and He intended for it to continue whether Abraham lived up to his part of the bargain or not. Regardless of man's action, God is determined to keep His part of the agreement. He ratified that covenant, and once a contract is ratified, it cannot be altered by only one of the two parties involved.

If this is true, then our actions, our breach of contract, still does not disannul the agreement. It takes both parties to disannul it. Despite the many times we may have fallen down on our part, God still has not agreed with us to void our contract. Therefore, our sin does not alter our covenant relationship with our Father through the Lord Jesus Christ. Our sins and shortcomings do not invalidate our contractual agreement. We are still the righteousness of God in Christ. We're still well, healed, prosperous, and endowed with eternal life.

"Oh, but I'm not well."

That's because you haven't been taking full advantage of the covenant. It's still in force. Your sickness doesn't disannul the contract. Neither does your sin or your poverty or even your death. The covenant still stands. God Himself will not change it. If you're not enjoying all the blessings of your covenant with God, then you don't need a new contract, you just need to avail yourself of the full benefits of the one you already have. You do it the same way you became a party to the agreement in the first place, through faith.

3:18 For if the inheritance *is* of the law, *it is* no longer of promise; but God gave *it* to Abraham by promise.

The coming of the law did not annul the promises of the covenant. The blessing wasn't given to Abraham by the law; that came 430 years later. The blessing was given to Abraham by promise.

Suppose I promise to give my brother a hundred dollars after church services, and suppose he agrees to accept that gift. Whose obligation is it to fulfill that agreement? His or mine? It's mine, because I was the one who made the promise. I'm not obligated by law but by our agreement. God made promises to Abraham. The obligation to fulfill those promises was not Abraham's, but God's. This has nothing to do with law, but with agreement.

If God has promised to bless us, and we have agreed to receive that blessing, then whose obligation is it to fulfill the agreement, ours or God's? It's God's. What is our part? To receive the blessing. God is obligated to keep

His Word of promise to us. We are only obligated to receive the benefit of that promise by simply reaching out and taking it. God promises, we receive, and that settles it.

Then why do we feel we have to do something to receive our healing or prosperity or success or any of the other good things promised us in God's Word? Just like God's gift of salvation, all that is required of us it to exercise faith to receive.

We said it was by "the grace of our Lord Jesus Christ, that, though he was rich, yet for [our] sakes he became poor, that [we] through his poverty might be rich" (2 Corinthians 8:9). What are riches? A grace. We also said that God made Christ, who knew no sin, to be made sin for us; that we might be made the righteousness of God in him (2 Corinthians 5:21). What is righteousness then? A grace. We read that God laid on Jesus all our sicknesses and infirmities so that by His death on the cross we might be made whole and healthy (Isaiah 53:4–5). What is health? What is wholeness? A grace of God.

Grace is unmerited favor. It is favor given, not because it is deserved but because of the mercy and love of the giver. All the promises of the covenant are graces, gifts of God. Abraham was declared righteous, not by what he did, but simply because he believed God, "being fully persuaded that, what he had promised, he was able also to perform" (Romans 4:21).

The giving of the covenant was accomplished by God. The confirming of the covenant was accomplished by God. The fulfillment of the covenant was accomplished by Christ. The keeping of the promises of the covenant is up to our heavenly Father. What then is our part? Our part in the covenant is to reap the benefits of it! How do we do that? Through faith. We simply believe we have received, as our Lord told us in Mark 11:24. God provides; we appropriate.

3:19 ¶ What purpose then *does* the law *serve*? It was added because of transgressions, till the Seed should come to whom the promise was made; *and it was* appointed through angels by the hand of a mediator.

If all this is true, then what was the purpose of the law? If Abraham, Isaac, Jacob, and Joseph all survived without it all those centuries, why was it given at all?

If the law was "added," does this mean it was added to the Abrahamic covenant? No, that would be illegal: No "man disannulleth, or addeth thereto" (v. 15). The Mosaic law could not be an addition to the Abrahamic covenant, not in the sense of an amendment to that covenant. It was simply a tool used by God in addition to (along with) the covenant. It was not itself a part of that covenant, nor was it ever meant to disannul or alter the original agreement between God and man. Then why was it added?

. . . Because of transgressions, . . .

The law was added because of man's transgressions. This word translated "transgressions" simply means sins. The purpose of the law was to point out man's violation of the covenant agreement. Had there been no law, man would never have been conscious of what God expected of him or how he had failed to live up to that expectation.

. . . Till the seed should come . . .

"Seed" is singular. Who is the seed of Abraham? Jesus Christ. The law was added only until Jesus Christ came. Then He put it away. He did that, not by destroying (abolishing) it, but by fulfilling it (Matthew 5:17). Since Christ fulfilled the law, you and I are no longer subject to that law. It's not for today. It was given to Moses until the coming of the seed, the Lord Jesus Christ, who would fulfill it in every detail.

In Romans 5, Paul touches on this subject of the law. Notice how he begins verse 20: "Moreover the law entered." This word "entered" is a stage term taken from the Greek theater. It was used to indicate the action of a supporting actor who came on stage to perform until the lead actor made his entrance, at which time the supporting actor retired from the stage.

Paul applied this term to the Mosaic law, likening it to a minor player whose role is simply to set the stage for the entrance of the principal player. The law came on the scene at the time of Moses. It remained on stage only until the arrival of Jesus Christ. Then it gave place to Him, never to reappear. The law was introduced by Moses; it exited with the Lord Jesus Christ. It has no bearing on us today because its role in the drama of life was completed.

Now while He was hanging suspended on the cross, our Lord made seven statements. One of them was, "It is finished" (John 19:30). There is a very popular doctrine among many Christians today advanced by a well-known and widely read theologian of the past. This teaching holds that when Christ said, "It is finished," He was referring to the Abrahamic covenant. I do not agree. He was not speaking of the covenant; rather, He was referring to the Mosaic law. In Colossians 2:14, Paul told us "Blotting out the handwriting of ordinances that was against us, which was contrary to us . . . [Christ] took it out of the way, nailing it to his cross." Our Lord took the law, the "handwriting of ordinances," and crucified it by nailing it to the cross. Jesus said He did not come to destroy the law, but to fulfill it. He did that by being nailed to the cross Himself, by taking the curse of the law upon Himself. When He had suffered the full penalty of the curse, He had then fulfilled all righteousness. Therefore the law is like a check that has been paid and canceled. It is no longer valid. All it serves as now is proof that the debt has been paid in full.

The Abrahamic covenant, with its blessing, is still in effect. It will be fulfilled at the second coming of the Lord Jesus Christ to establish His millennial kingdom on earth.

. . . To whom the promise was made; . . .

This phrase reckons back to the time when the covenant was first made between God and Abraham and his seed. That seed was Jesus Christ. The promises were given to Abraham and Jesus. Christ fulfilled our part of that covenant when He went to the cross. God has fulfilled His part by giving us (through Christ our representative) His "great and precious promises" (2 Peter 1:4). We are in covenant relationship with our heavenly Father. In Christ our divine substitute, we are pleasing to God. We also qualify to receive, by faith, the full benefits of sonship.

The law was not given to provide salvation, but to serve as a sign pointing toward salvation. That salvation is found only in the seed to whom the promises were given, the Lord Jesus Christ. No one can come to the Father except by Him (John 14:6). For it was only through Him that man's part in the covenant found fulfillment. Anyone who rejects what Christ has done for him personally on the cross of Calvary disqualifies himself from the blessing of the covenant. He is left to try and attain right standing with God on his own merit, and no one can do that. That's why Paul urged the Galatians not to withdraw from grace to follow after the illusion of salvation through works of the law. The law was never designed to save, only to point to Christ. Outside of Him, not only is there no salvation, there's not even any hope of salvation.

3:20 Now a mediator does not *mediate* for one *only*, but God is one.

3:21-29 The Law — Our Schoolmaster

I. The Law and the Promises (21–22)

3:21 ¶ *Is* the law then against the promises of God? Certainly not! For if there had been a law given which could have given life, truly righteousness would have been by the law.

Is the law then against the promises of God? . . .

No, the law is not in opposition to the promises; it complements them. The purpose of the Abrahamic covenant was to bring righteousness by faith. The law was added to point people to the covenant. God would not give us two guides in opposition to each other. That would be confusing. God is not the author of confusion, but of order. When people were so blinded by their sin they couldn't see, they needed the righteousness by faith provided by the Abrahamic covenant. The law was given to turn their eyes to that covenant. But the law could only point to righteousness; it could not provide it of itself. If the law had provided righteousness, then there would have been no need of a savior.

3:22 But the Scripture has confined all under sin, that the promise by faith in Jesus Christ might be given to those who believe.

This point is also brought out in Romans 3:23: "For all have sinned, and come short of the glory of God." This is a reference to Deuteronomy 27:26, "Cursed be he that confirmeth not all the words of this law to do them." Since it is obvious no one can ever keep every word of the law, then everyone is concluded under sin, even under the old covenant. Therefore, no one is justified by keeping the law, because no one can keep it. If a person were to keep every jot and tittle of the law, he wouldn't need the law to make him perfect, he would already be perfect. So again we see that the law does not make perfect; it only serves to emphasize human imperfection.

When Galatians 3:22 says all have been concluded under sin, it is not referring to any specific sin, such as adultery, lying, cheating, stealing, or murder. Notice, this word "sin" is in the singular. Whenever the Bible speaks of sin in this way, it is referring to the sin nature, the flesh.

Most of the time, you and I don't commit sins because we are helpless victims of some evil spirit that gets hold of us. We commit sins because we have a nature called the flesh. It is this fleshly nature that continually pushes us toward sinfulness. When we became new creatures in Christ, we received a new Spirit within that has power over the flesh. That's why John reminded us He who is in us is greater than he who is in the world (1 John 4:4). Now that we are born again of the Spirit of God, our inward man, our spiritual nature, is stronger than the nature of the outward man of the flesh.

Am I saying we have two natures within us (in our spirit) that are always warring against each other? No, the struggle is the recreated spirit at war with the outward body, the flesh. The only time they war against each other is when we get out of the will of God, when we get carnal. As long as we remain in fellowship with God, the greater power can put down the lesser power. If we are truly spiritual, when our flesh rises up in opposition to our spirits, our spirits take dominion over the flesh, and that ends the rebellion.

I have often heard people describe the battle between the flesh and spirit of a believer like a person who has two dogs on the inside, a white one and a black one. These two animals are always fighting one another, and the one that will win is the one you feed, because he gets stronger and stronger. But that is not really so. We Christians don't have two fighting dogs inside of us. What we have is a living man and a dead man. It is only when we get out of fellowship with the Lord that the dead man resurrects to cause us trouble. As long as we are walking and living in the Spirit, we are dead to the flesh (Romans 6:11).

In his letter to the Christians in Rome, Paul dealt extensively with this concept of sin versus the spirit. Very little of the book of Romans has to do with personal sins; rather, it deals with the sin nature, or the nature of the flesh. Sins like stealing, lying, and killing are only the symptoms of sin. Sin itself is not an act; it's not even an attitude. Sin is a nature that drives a person to think, speak, and do things contrary to the nature of God. That is the whole theme of the seventh chapter of Romans. Paul described how he came to realize there was a force driving him to do what his recreated spirit did not want to do.

In essence Paul said, "I don't understand it. Why is it that I keep doing the things I don't want to do and failing to do the things I want to do? I want to do right, but somehow I always end up doing wrong. Why is that? Why am I so mixed up inside?" One day he discovered the reason: "Oh, it's because my flesh is warring against my mind!" No doubt he recalled the words of Jesus in Matthew 26:41 when He told His disciples to watch and pray because "the spirit indeed is willing, but the flesh is weak." This word "willing" is more than just agreeable, it means "desirous."

What our Lord was saying was the spirit desires to do right, but the flesh is not strong enough to fulfill the righteous desires of the spirit. That's exactly what Paul discovered. He realized by looking at his weaknesses, sins, and failures, he had been focusing his attention on the symptoms (the acts of the flesh) instead of the real cause of his problem (the flesh itself).

God gives us a new nature when we are born again. How effective that new nature is in controlling our lives depends upon how much attention we give to it, and how closely we keep in fellowship with our heavenly Father. Neglect of our spiritual lives produces the same results as neglect of our physical bodies. If we want to remain strong and healthy physically so our bodies throw off the germs and viruses, we must give our bodies proper rest, nourishment, and exercise. So it is with our spiritual man. If we are to maintain dominion over the carnal nature, we must develop our spiritual nature through rest (meditation), nourishment (Bible reading, prayer, hearing the Word), and exercise (living out our faith daily). We don't do these things to please God, we do them to build up our inward man. These activities don't make us righteous; they just make us strong!

The scripture hath concluded all under sin . . .

The word "sin" here means the sin nature. This verse is speaking specifically about unbelievers, although believers still possess the nature of the flesh after the new birth. The believer has something to fight back with, the power of the Holy Spirit inside him.

Some people seem to have the mistaken idea that when they were born again, they were relieved of the flesh. That is obviously not so. We Christians were born again spiritually, but as long as we are on this earth, we will be living in the flesh. Didn't Paul himself refer to this truth when he wrote in this same letter, "The life which I now live in the flesh I live by the faith of the Son of God" (Galatians 2:20)?

I believe in sanctification. But sanctification does not come overnight. It is not instantaneous; rather, it is progressive. There is no such thing as "one-shot" sanctification by which a person becomes born again and never sins again as long as he lives. Some Christians go around confessing that since they are the righteousness of God in Christ, they no longer sin. That's self-delusion. It's also hypocritical. We all have the potential to sin. That's why we have 1 John 1:9. We can confess our sins and receive forgiveness. (That scripture was written to believers, not unbelievers.)

Sanctification is twofold: spiritual and physical. Spiritually we are sanctified the moment we were born again of the Spirit of God. However, physical sanctification, righteous living in the flesh, takes longer. It is a process we begin at the moment of new birth, but it lasts as long as we live on this earth. In essence, we are sanctified spiritually so we can begin to live a sanctified life in the flesh. That's what Paul meant when he said the life he lived in the flesh, he lived by the faith of the Son of God.

Some people have sanctification backwards. They're trying to live a good life so they can be born again. That's wrong, too. It'll never work. We are born again to live a good life. Unless we are first sanctified by the Spirit of God, we have no power to live a truly sanctified life in the flesh. It is the presence and power of the greater one within us that gives us dominion and authority over our fleshly, carnal nature.

. . . That the promise by faith of Jesus Christ might be given to them that believe.

This is a mistranslation. It should read: "That the promise by faith *in* Jesus Christ might be given to them that believe." How do we receive the promises of God? It's by putting our faith *in* Jesus Christ.

II. Kept under the Law (23–25)

3:23 But before faith came, we were kept under guard by the law, kept for the faith which would afterward be revealed.

But before faith came, we were kept under the law . . .

This word "kept" means guarded. Before faith came, we were guarded by a jailer, the law. We were in prison.

. . . Shut up unto the faith which should afterwards be revealed.

The prison in which we were shut up was our own sin nature. The jailer who kept us in that prison of our fleshly nature was the law, just as it is the law that keeps inmates shut away in our state and federal prisons today. The difference is inmates in criminal institutions know they are behind bars; we didn't know we were prisoners of the law. That's why Paul is having such a hard time convincing the Galatians they are now free; they don't know they are in bondage. Once they had been in bondage to sin and heathenism. Now they are in bondage to the law. They went from one form of bondage to another. They had allowed themselves to come into bondage by subjecting themselves to the law that Christ came to fulfill for them.

That's why Paul is so upset. They don't realize the purpose of the law is only to expose sin, to reveal to people they are in bondage, so they canbe set free by faith in Christ Jesus. By turning from faith to the law, the Galatians are doing just the opposite of what God had intended. He hadn't sent the law to regulate believers; He sent it to lead sinners to Christ. Now that they are in Christ, the Galatians have no need of the law. It fulfilled its purpose when Christ came and fulfilled it.

Yet so many people don't seem to understand this principle, even today. Many times, the hardest people to witness to about Christ are not sinners who know nothing of righteousness; it is religious people who think righteousness is something they attain by their own efforts. It is very hard to set free a person who doesn't even know he's in prison. Such people think by keeping religious rules and regulations, they are becoming justified in the eyes of God. The law keeps them shut up in prison, in spiritual bondage. It is only when they finally realize the absolute impossibility of keeping all those codes that they are ever willing to accept God's free gift of justification and redemption through simple faith in His Son Jesus Christ.

3:24 Therefore the law was our tutor *to bring us* to Christ, that we might be justified by faith.

Wherefore the law was our schoolmaster . . .

"Wherefore" means in conclusion. Paul begins to draw this part of his argument to a close. The word "schoolmaster" is understood today, but still gives a wrong impression of what Paul was trying to say. When we see that word, we instantly think of a schoolteacher, an instructor in a public or private educational institution. That's not what a schoolmaster was to the people in Paul's day. The Greek word translated "schoolmaster" here in the *King James Version* is *paidagogos* (*paidos*, a boy + *agogos*, leading = boy-leading). It is from this word that we derive our English word *pedagogue*, meaning "*a teacher.*" However, in the culture of the ancient Greeks, a *pedagogue* was a household servant, often a slave. His role was that of tutor-overseer. He was charged with the responsibility of watching over, caring for, training, and instructing the boy child of the family until the son became of age. At that time, the *pedagogue* was relieved of his duties, and the son took full responsibility for his own actions.

. . . To bring us unto Christ, that we might be justified by faith.

What then was the purpose of the law? The law was our *pedagogue*. It was a servant of our Father, employed by Him to lead us to Christ Jesus that we might be justified by faith in Him. Notice, the law itself did not bring faith; it led people to the person of Christ through whom justification was received by faith.

3:25 But after faith has come, we are no longer under a tutor.

Since Christ has come to earth, died, been resurrected, and ascended to heaven where He now sits at the right hand of God the Father, where does that leave the law, our pedagogue? It has accomplished its task, discharged its duties, fulfilled its purpose. Therefore it is dismissed. It no longer has authority or jurisdiction over those of us who are in Christ Jesus. Once you and I came to Jesus, our former pedagogue was no longer needed. When we were born again, our pedagogue was dismissed, and we became responsible for our own lives. Now that we have reached spiritual manhood, for us to go back and try to submit to a system of dos and don'ts is to submit ourselves to a former slave and have him take care of us. Not only is that foolish, it is a denial of our rights as sons.

Then why do people do that? Having once attained their spiritual maturity, why do believers try to return to a system of rules and regulations? One basic reason is laziness. It's easier to follow a set of laws than to think for yourself.

A second reason is fear. Many Christians are so insecure, they want someone to tell them exactly what to think, say, and do. They are afraid of the responsibility that comes with freedom. It's sort of like working all your life for someone else rather than striking out on your own to run your own business.

Most people prefer the security of being an employee to the freedom and responsibility that goes with being their own master. That may be fine in the work market, but it is dangerous in the spiritual realm. There are always those who are happy to appoint themselves as religious leaders and to take advantage of the insecurity of immature believers. That's one reason for all the cults inside the church as well as outside. Christians need to learn to take seriously their responsibility as full-grown sons. Part of that responsibility is the duty to think for themselves.

III. Complete in Christ (26–29)

3:26 ¶ For you are all sons of God through faith in Christ Jesus.

For ye are all the children of God by faith in Christ Jesus.

This word translated "children" is the Greek word *huios*, which we said was closer to our word sons than to children. *Teknon* usually refers to the physical Jews, whereas *huios* denotes those who have exercised faith in Christ. Paul is telling us we are all sons of God. This word indicates we are mature sons not little children under the care of a pedagogue.

Now in this passage, Paul presents spiritual or positional truth rather than temporal, earthly truth. Positionally, the moment you and I accept Jesus Christ as our savior, God sees us as mature. In Colossians Paul used the word "complete": "And ye are complete in him [Christ], which is the head of all principality and power" (Colossians 2:10). At the precise moment we were born again, God saw us complete. Where? In Christ. How did we get into that position of completeness? We entered that state through faith. The moment we became "in him," we became complete.

Now you may not feel mature, complete, or righteous. You may remember all too well those unrighteous acts that prove beyond a shadow of a doubt you are not mature or complete or righteous. But you must remember those acts do not make you unrighteous any more than your works of the law make you righteous. If your righteousness came not by works, but through faith, then your wrong acts do not destroy your righteousness, not in the eyes of God. Therefore they shouldn't destroy your righteousness, maturity, and completeness in your own eyes.

It is much easier to walk in righteousness once you realize God sees you that way. Once you fix your eyes on your goal, the pathway to that goal becomes clearer and easier to follow. Always keep foremost in your mind that in Jesus Christ you are complete, not because of anything you do or have done but because you have been granted His completeness. When God looks at you, He sees Jesus Christ. Therefore you are everything He is (1 John 4:17).

Then if you will fix your eyes and set your affection on things above, you will see that anything you are striving to become in this life, you have already attained. You're already there. It's so much easier to act righteous when you realize you're already righteous. It's much easier to act sanctified when you realize God already sees you sanctified. It's much easier to act mature when you know God sees you as a mature person.

The key to spiritual maturity is positional truth, you having already become that which you aspire to be.

Paul tells us we are the mature sons of God by faith in Christ Jesus. When did that happen? The answer is found in the next verse:

3:27 For as many of you as were baptized into Christ have put on Christ.

We became the mature sons of God when we are baptized into Christ Jesus. Now note the expression "put on Christ." This will be discussed more in detail in chapter 4 of Galatians.

3:28 There is neither Jew nor Greek, there is neither slave nor free, there is neither male nor female; for you are all one in Christ Jesus.

In verse 24, we learned about the pedagogue. In verse 26, we learned we are mature sons. In verse 27, we found we have "put on" Christ. Now here in verse 28, we discover that in Christ there is no distinction between the Jew and the non-Jew, the bond and the free, the male and the female. Again Paul is speaking in spiritual terms. Obviously in the natural, physical realm there will always be distinctions made between the races, social classes, and sexes but not in the spiritual realm. In Christ we are all one.

3:29 And if you *are* Christ's, then you are Abraham's seed, and heirs according to the promise.

Notice, we are "Abraham's seed." This word "seed" is in the singular. Do you recall from verse 16 to whom the promises of God were given in the Abrahamic covenant? "Now to Abraham and his seed were the promises made." In that verse, the seed was the Lord Jesus Christ. Paul told us if we are in Christ, we are the seed. How can that be?

The answer is very simple. When God made promises to Abraham and his seed, Christ was there in spirit (though He would not be born in flesh for hundreds of years). Yet Christ was not participating in that covenant agreement on His own behalf, He was there on our behalf. The promises were made by God to Abraham and Christ, but Christ had no need of these promises. He only participated as our representative. Everything He did was for us. In reality, the promises made by God to Abraham and his seed were actually made to Abraham and us. That's where we came into the Abrahamic covenant. How did we get into it? By faith. Because we are Abraham's seed through faith in Jesus Christ, we are heirs according to the promise.

4:1–16 Paul's First Trip to Galatia

I. Our Redemption from the Law (1–5)

4:1–3 ¶ Now I say *that* the heir, as long as he is a child, does not differ at all from a slave, though he is master of all, 2 but is under guardians and stewards until the time appointed by the father. 3 Even so we, when we were children, were in bondage under the elements of the world.

In this opening passage, Paul likens us to an heir, born of the head of the house, who must serve a time under tutors and governors. These are types representing the law that kept us as our pedagogue until the time appointed by God for us to be given the full rights of manhood.

4:4 But when the fullness of the time had come, God sent forth His Son, born of a woman, born under the law,

The expression "born of a woman" refers to the virgin birth of our Lord. "Born under the law" indicates the Messiah was born under the law. In fact, Jesus Christ was born, lived His life, was crucified, died, was buried, was resurrected, and ascended into heaven, all under the dispensation of the law. The new dispensation (which is the church age) did not begin until the day of Pentecost with the outpouring of the Holy Spirit.

That's why you and I don't have to live by the law. We have the Holy Spirit living in us as our guide. Since we are in Christ, positionally speaking, we cannot become any more complete. Can Christ become any more mature? However, in our Christian walk, in this fleshly body, you and I do continue to grow and mature. We start out as babes in Christ, and by feeding on the sincere milk of the Word, we grow and develop until we are ready for meat. We grow in God's Word and learn to be led by the Spirit of God Himself. That's when we become full-grown sons of God: "For as many as are led by the Spirit of God, they are the sons of God" (Romans 8:14). Holy Spirit leadership is a sign of spiritual maturity.

Some people tell me, "Oh, I wish I knew how to be led by the Spirit." I ask them how they make decisions. "Oh, when I'm faced with some problem or circumstance in my life, I just go by the scriptures. Usually some verse or passage will come to my mind and I'll apply it to my situation."

"Then you are being led of the Spirit. The Spirit of God always leads in line with the Word of God. The Spirit has been sent to lead and guide us into all Truth (the Word)."

"Oh, but that's so simple. I thought God would speak through some great prophet or dream or vision or unusual event."

He can speak that way, and sometimes He does. But most of the time, God speaks to His children just as He spoke to His prophet Elijah: not in the strong wind or the earthquake or the fire, but in a still small voice (1 Kings 19:11–12). That's why, in the midst of all the busy activity of our daily lives and even in our exuberant worship, we still need a time to be still and know He is God. Too often we're seeking some great manifestation, some overwhelming pronouncement or personal prophecy, some miraculous or spectacular occurrence, when we should be simply listening for the gentle, sweet voice of the Spirit. The truly mature son of God hears more in silence than the frenzied crowd hears in a trumpet blast.

4:5 to redeem those who were under the law, that we might receive the adoption as sons.

Jesus Christ came to redeem those who were under the law first. Who was that? The Jews. Then Paul goes on to say, "that we might receive the adoption of sons." When he uses the pronoun "we," he is talking about himself and the Galatians to whom he is writing. Christ came to redeem not just the Jews but the Gentiles as well, everyone. Jesus came to the Jew first, then the Gentile.

Isaiah spoke for the whole of mankind when he said, "All we like sheep have gone astray; we have turned every one to his own way; and the LORD hath laid on him [Christ] the iniquity of us all" (Isaiah 53:6). Whether they had the law or not, whether they tried to keep the law or not, all mankind was lost, condemned, without hope, until Christ came to give His life as a ransom for many.

What was the threefold curse of the law? Sickness, poverty, and spiritual death. Everyone, Jew and Gentile alike, was subject to that curse. Everyone, both Jew and Gentile, needed redemption through Jesus Christ. Jesus came to redeem all those who were under the curse of the law, which was all mankind: "For all have sinned, and come short of the glory of God" (Romans 3:23). He came to redeem the whole world. Jews were under the law and couldn't keep it. Gentiles were under the curse even though they did not have the law. Everyone needed redemption. Redemption came in the form of the Messiah who was sent by God so "that we might receive the adoption as sons."

II. Our Adoption as Sons

This phrase about being adopted as the sons of God is one of the most misunderstood in the whole Bible. Most Christians don't have the foggiest idea of what it really means. Even pastors and teachers of the Word sometimes miss the whole point of Paul's analogy here. I once read a book in which the author used this text as evidence for his theory that when a person is saved by faith, he is just a sinner who has been adopted by God; he is not really God's blood relative. That is totally false. Nothing could be further from the truth.

Jesus told Nicodemus that in order to enter the kingdom of heaven, a person must be "born again" (John 3:3). Paul told us, "If any man be in Christ, he is a new creature: old things are passed away; behold, all things are become new" (2 Corinthians 5:17). If we become Christians by being born again, and are totally new creatures, then it is ridiculous to say we are just sinners who have been adopted by God. I'm not just an old sinner saved by grace. Neither are you, not if you are in Christ Jesus. We used to be sinners, but now, according to 2 Corinthians 5:21, we have become the righteousness of God in Christ. We are now the sons of God, and I can assure you God doesn't have any sinners in His family. We're not sinners; we're saints and became saints when we were washed in the blood of Jesus.

Paul didn't say believers are adopted sinners. He told us we are the very sons of God: "For as many as are led by the Spirit of God, they are the sons of God. For ye have not received the spirit of bondage again to fear; but ye have received the Spirit of adoption, whereby we cry, Abba, Father. The Spirit itself beareth witness with our spirit, that we are the children of God: and if children, then heirs; heirs of God, and joint-heirs with Christ" (Romans 8:14–17).

"If we are the sons of God, then why did Paul speak of our 'adoption' as sons?"

When Paul used the term "adoption," it had a totally different meaning to the New Testament Greeks than it does to us Americans. We think of adoption as taking a child from outside the family and making him a son by legal means. Such a child is not a true blood offspring. Throughout the New Testament the word adoption referred to the action of parents who "adopted" their own children into the family. Let me explain.

The Greek word translated "adoption" in the *King James Version* is *huiothesia*. It is a compound word made up of two elements that literally mean son-placing (in the sense of adult son placing.) It was used to refer to the ceremony in which a minor son was formally initiated into full family status by being vested with the rights and privileges of an adult.

To the Greeks, adoption didn't convey the image of taking a child from outside the family and bringing him into it by a legal process. Rather, it symbolized maturity, the imparting of the full rights of sonship upon a minor child who was already a member of the family.

In the time of Paul, a boy child born into a Greek family was considered a ward of his appointed pedagogue who exercised authority over him. The pedagogue was charged with the responsibility of teaching and training the boy until the time he was ready to accept full responsibility for himself, which was usually at about the age of 14. Until that time, the child, though he was heir to his father's name and estate, was totally subject to his pedagogue. Though a son for all practical purposes, he had no more rights or privileges than a slave in the household.

Until the boy reached the age of consent, he was required to wear a cloak of childhood to indicate to others he was not yet responsible for his own actions and decisions. When he had attained sufficient maturity to take care of himself, the boy was presented to the head of the family by his *pedagogue* as a candidate for adoption. If he successfully demonstrated his maturity, he then went through a ceremony called the *toga virilis*, which means the ceremony of the cloak of manhood. His cloak of childhood was formally removed from his shoulders, and he was invested with the cloak of manhood.

With that ceremony, the boy became a man. Henceforth, he was no longer just a child, a servant under a pedagogue. He was a son, an heir of the father, with all the rights and privileges that went with that title.

This is what Paul was referring to in this passage about our adoption as sons by God the Father: "wherefore thou art no more a servant, but a son; and if a son, then an heir of God through Christ."

What happened to the pedagogue after the boy had been declared a man? He was no longer needed. His task had been completed. He was assigned a new charge. Never again would he be placed in a position of authority and dominion over the son.

That's what happens in our case. When we accept Christ into our lives, when we "put on" Christ (our cloak of manhood), our pedagogue (the law) was dismissed. It no longer has authority or dominion over us because we are full-fledged sons of the Father. It still remains, but now it pertains only to those who are still under its jurisdiction, those who have not yet come to the Father through faith in Jesus Christ. The law is for the unrighteous (1 Timothy 1:9–10).

III. No More Servants, but Sons (6–7)

4:6 ¶ And because you are sons, God has sent forth the Spirit of His Son into your hearts, crying out, "Abba, Father!"

Now if you are a woman, you may be thinking, "How can I be a 'son' of God?" You are just as much a son of God as any man, because this word simply indicates a mature offspring. Paul already told us that in Christ there is neither Jew nor Greek, bond nor free, male nor female (Galatians 3:28). We are all one in the body of Christ. If that is so, then we don't need to join movements to fight for our rights, either as males or females. All we need to do is to recognize the freedom and equality that is already ours through our Lord Jesus Christ. There is no one as free as the person who walks in line with the Word of God and in harmony with His Spirit, for the one whom the Son has set free is free indeed (John 8:36).

This word *Abba* is Chaldean for father, just as the Greek word *pater* here was translated father. Some people seem to think *Abba* has some deep, mystical significance. They go around chanting it as though it is a sort of magic word that somehow moves them closer to God. All Paul did here was repeat the same word in two different languages. The Chaldean word *Abba* was simply left untranslated. We cry, "Father, Father."

4:7 Therefore you are no longer a slave but a son, and if a son, then an heir of God through Christ.

There is an implied intimacy with God here, the kind that allows us to call Him "Daddy" as well as "Father." The people under the old covenant could not do that. Until the coming of the Holy Spirit to live in the individual believer, no Jew ever looked upon himself as a son of God. This new relationship between God and man was what Jesus was preparing the Jews for when He began to teach His disciples to address God as their heavenly Father. Prior to this time, no one had dared to approach God that way. He was not their Father; He was Elohim, the Almighty, the Eternal; He was Creator, Lord, Sovereign. Yet Jesus began to give them a glimpse of the new relationship that would be theirs once they had become participants in the new covenant God was establishing with them through Him.

The truth Paul is sharing with the Galatians is that when they received the Spirit of Christ into their hearts, they too become the children of God. No longer are they servants, but sons. If they are sons of God, as Jesus is the Son of God, they are heirs of God just as Jesus is. The way they become sons and heirs is by being born again of the Spirit of God.

It was previously stated that the Old Testament saints were saved, but were not born again until after Pentecost; no one could be born of the Spirit of God until the Spirit had been given to all mankind. At Pentecost the Spirit didn't come exclusively upon those in the upper room; He came upon all who had put their trust in God through Jesus Christ His Son. The same Spirit is still with us today, He has never left. He is still bearing children of divinity, still giving birth to new sons of God. He is still filling believers with His presence and power.

In the Old Testament, no one was a son of God because the only way to come into the family of God is by birth, the new birth. Moses, as great as he was, was not a son of God; he was a servant in the household of God (Hebrews 3:5). Elijah, the great prophet, was not a son of God, but only a servant of the Most High.

When Jesus Christ arose from the dead, He became the firstborn of many brethren (Romans 8:29). He ascended into heaven and poured out the Holy Spirit upon those who had believed on Him. The Holy Spirit began in Jerusalem and encircled the globe, bringing believers into the family of God.

John said of Jesus Christ, "As many as received him, to them gave he power to become the sons of God, even to them that believe on his name" (John 1:12). John does not say Jesus made sons of God out of those who believed in Him; He only gave them "power to become the sons of God." That event took place after Jesus had returned to His Father in heaven. It was not Jesus who made His followers into sons of God; it was the Holy Spirit who gave them new birth. They had the power to become sons of God by their faith in Christ. In one sense, they had their ticket to sonship by faith, but they had to hold onto that ticket until the day of Pentecost when they presented it for admission into the family of God. Rebirth came through the "washing of regeneration, and renewing of the Holy Ghost" (Titus 3:5).

"And if a son, then an heir of God through Christ" (Galatians 5:7). That new birth brought with it a new relationship to God. No longer were they servants of the Most High; now they were sons of God. He was no longer just Creator and Lord; now He was also their heavenly Father.

I imagine one of the things the followers of Jesus were saying on the day of Pentecost as they burst forth into praises to God in their new tongues was, "Abba, Father!" That's why I always try to get new converts to say to God, "Lord, thank You for saving me; now I can call You Father." That gives the new believer a whole new perspective of God and of himself. He begins to see God as His loving heavenly Father rather than a faraway, all powerful being. He also sees himself differently from then on. No longer is he a mere subject, or servant of the Lord God Jehovah; he has become a son of God, an heir of God and a joint heir with Christ.

If Jesus is the heir of God, and if we believers are joint heirs with Him, what is it we are heirs of? "All things" (Hebrews 1:2).

When you and I were born again, born into the family of God, we went through a spiritual ceremony of *toga virilis.* Our cloak of childhood was removed and the cloak of mature sonship was placed upon us. From that moment on, we were declared by God to be full-grown sons, heirs to all that is His. We can see this inheritance illustrated in the parable of the Prodigal Son. Do you remember what the loving father told the older brother who was angry because his younger brother had received such a welcome home after "wasting his inheritance"? "Son, thou art ever with me, and all that I have is thine" (Luke 15:31). That's the way it is with us as the sons of God: all He has is ours (1 Corinthians 3:21–23).

Wouldn't it be foolish if we, after having been granted the freedom and fullness of sonship, would suddenly decide to go back, take upon ourselves the cloak of childhood, and deliberately place ourselves under the authority and dominion of our old pedagogue, the law? Yet that is precisely what the Galatians were doing. How stupid. They had just been brought out of bondage to sin — just been set free from the law of sin and death, just been received into the family of God as heirs of all that is His — only to turn right around and place themselves back under bondage. This kind of ignorance and foolishness Paul just could not understand.

IV. Why Turn Back to Bondage? (8–9)

4:8 ⁋ But then, indeed, when you did not know God, you served those which by nature are not gods.

This expression "by nature" simply means in essence. Paul was asking these people, "How is it that when you were sinners, in essence you served those things that are not gods at all?" Before their conversion to Christ, the Galatians were heathens; they were idol worshippers. They bowed down and worshipped images carved from wood and stone. Of course, we know that man-made gods are not gods at all. Yet notice Paul didn't say they worshipped non-gods; he said they "served" them. That is, the Galatians served idols. To serve something is to be a servant or slave of that thing.

Paul was telling these people that before they came to know Christ, they were slaves; they were in bondage. As Gentiles, they were never in bondage to the Jewish law; rather, they were slaves to the law of sin and death. They were under condemnation because they had not believed on Him who has the power to set men free, the power to cause them to become the sons of God.

4:9 But now after you have known God, or rather are known by God, how *is it that* you turn again to the weak and beggarly elements, to which you desire again to be in bondage?

Now that you have come to know God through His Son Jesus Christ —now that He has set you free from the law of sin and death — why do you turn back to another form of death, the law? Once you were in bondage, trapped by your ignorance of God and His love. Now that Christ has delivered you from that trap, why do you want to turn back to another form of enslavement?

To Paul, what the Galatians are doing makes no sense at all. He can't understand why anyone who was once set free from the bondage of heathenism would ever want to fall into the bondage of Judaism. One is as bad as the other. Both are forms of bondage, forms of religion, man's puny efforts to gain spiritual favor and right standing by giving service to a dead system of physical rules and regulations.

Paul is much too intelligent and enlightened to be fooled into thinking external rules could ever produce a new internal spirit. He knows the only way man can ever truly please God is by becoming one with Him through the new birth. Once that happens, once the person has become a true son of God by spiritual rebirth, then he is no longer a slave to a system of external rules. From then on he is led from the inside by the indwelling Spirit of God.

V. Led of the Spirit, Not by the Law (10)

4:10 You observe days and months and seasons and years.

Here Paul begins to rebuke the Galatians for allowing the legalistic Judaizers to influence them into observing the Jewish calendar instead of holding fast to the freedom that was won for them through the suffering of the
Lord Jesus. The "days" the Galatians were observing were Jewish Sabbath
days. These Gentiles in Galatia had become Sabbath-keepers. Remember,
this is Saturday, not Sunday, the Christian day of rest and worship.

Remember how legalistic the Jews had become about keeping the Sabbath? Through the centuries they had worked out an elaborate and complicated system of laws regulating every possible aspect of Sabbath-keep-
ing. For example, they had determined the exact number of steps allowed
to be taken on the Sabbath without constituting work. They had become
so minutely involved in keeping the law, they had missed the whole point
of it. They actually broke the Sabbath by trying to keep it because they
worked so hard trying to avoid work. They also worked very hard at trying
to force their own self-righteous standards on everyone else. They had
succeeded in making the law a stumbling block instead of a stepping-stone.

That kind of legalistic attitude and behavior did not die out with the ancient Jews. I remember well when I was growing up how strictly many
Christians kept the Lord's Day. There were laws about what could and
couldn't be done on Sunday just like the Pharisees had about Saturday.
Christians were not supposed to do any kind of work for any reason on
Sunday. They couldn't even play baseball. Of course, you wouldn't dare
think of going hunting or fishing or even swimming on Sunday (especially
not in mixed company) and moviegoing was definitely out.

I still cannot figure out why some perfectly legal activities six days a week
suddenly became such enormous sin on Sunday. The same roller skat-
ing rink that was a wholesome place of entertainment on Saturday night
somehow got devilishly transformed into a den of iniquity on Sunday af-
ternoon! But one thing was sure: If it was in any way restful, it wasn't
supposed to be done on the Day of Rest!

Then there were the blue laws. Some well-meaning souls somewhere obviously became so concerned about all the sinning going on every Lord's
Day, they decided it was their Christian duty to jump in and help God keep
it holy. They managed to get legislatures and city councils to pass strict
laws about what could and could not be sold on Sunday.

I remember going into a store in Kansas City on Sunday and seeing certain departments roped off because the religious zealots had come in to decide what was sinful to be sold. It was such a relief to see you could buy a baby bottle, but not detergent. I know the Lord was so grateful to those good church people for seeing to it that housewives in Kansas City could feed their babies on Sunday just as long as they weren't able to wash their dirty diapers!

Blue laws are a prime example of how the church of Jesus Christ has totally misunderstood its purpose and role on this earth. As Christians, we are called and commissioned to go into the entire world and spread the good news of Jesus Christ. We are not sent to tell businesses what they can and cannot sell on Sunday or any other day. We are ambassadors for Christ, not shelf inspectors!

Nor are we sin fighters. Our calling is not to fight sin; it's to save sinners. We don't have to spend our time and energy trying to close down bars and clubs. Once we get all the clientele of those establishments saved and filled to overflowing with the Holy Spirit, they will close themselves down because they won't have any customers to keep them going. The answer to alcoholism or drug addiction or prostitution is not prohibition; it's regeneration! If the church of Jesus Christ had ever worked as hard to fulfill the Great Commission as it had to stamp out sin, the whole world would be saved, and sin wouldn't be a problem anymore. I wonder how many souls have ever been saved from hell because some church group somewhere succeeded in forcing a neighborhood department store to close on Sunday?

In the church I pastor, we don't believe it is our duty to set out to close down the local shopping mall. Even if we managed to close it down, there would be no guarantee that either the merchants or their customers would be in church on Sunday. What merchant would want to go to a church that has just closed down his store? Besides that, we don't believe we have a right to try to force anyone to close his business to conform to our religious convictions. If we in the church of Jesus Christ want and expect our freedom to be respected, we must be very careful we are not guilty of depriving others of theirs, whether we agree with their beliefs or practices or not. Our church is persuaded that as Christians we have only one obligation, one responsibility to our fellow man, and that is to preach to him the glorious gospel of Jesus Christ. How can we effectivly preach if we are out picketing his store and driving away his customers?

It's high time we in the church come to our senses and quit trying to force our beliefs and practices onto others. It's high time we quit judging and condemning the world for not abiding by our standards of conscience or behavior. Why should they? They're lost. It wouldn't do them any good to abide by our codes anyway; it wouldn't save them. That's the whole point of this letter to the Galatians, the fact that no one is saved by keeping religious laws. Like Jesus, we're not sent to judge, but to save. The only way we'll ever save the world is not by condemning people for being sinners, but by loving them into becoming saints.

Finally, we Christians need to quit judging and condemning each other, regardless of our differences of doctrine and practice and belief. John had these strong words to say to the people of his day: "If a man say, I love God, and hateth his brother, he is a liar: for he that loveth not his brother whom he hath seen, how can he love God whom he hath not seen?" (1 John 4:20). Let's paraphrase that quote a bit: "If a Christian says, 'I love God,' and judges and condemns his fellow Christians, he is a liar: for how can he possibly love God whom he cannot see if he doesn't love his brothers and sisters in Christ whom he can see?" There will never be brotherhood among men until there is first brotherhood among brothers.

. . . and months, and times, and years.

"Months" refers to the fast initiated by the Jews during their Babylonian captivity. The Galatians have gone way back into Hebrew history to resurrect a commemoration that has nothing whatsoever to do with them personally. "Times" refers to the seven, regularly established Jewish feast days. The Galatians were observing Passover (the feast of Unleavened Bread), the dedication of the Firstfruits, and the feasts of Pentecost, Trumpets, Atonements, and Tabernacles. Can you see why Paul is so disgusted with these Gentiles? Why do they think they have to keep these Jewish commemorative feast days, none of which applied to them in its original context?

We can also see how foolish it was for Gentiles to allow legalistic Jews to intimidate them into trying to keep special observances that had no relation to them personally. We like to think we would not be so gullible as to let anyone put a religious straitjacket on us. Yet the same thing happens today. People come into a Christian church where they are born again and filled with the Spirit of God. Once set free from their bondage to the law of sin and death, many times they turn right around and fall into the trap of legalism. They will be taught now that they are free, they must give up the ways of the world and learn to abide by the way of the Word, usually as interpreted for them by some self-appointed religious leader or group.

The end result is things haven't changed at all. They are no more free in the church than they were outside it. Their lives are still bound by traditions, taboos, and thou-shalt-nots. They are told if they do not worship God in the prescribed manner, they are not spiritual. They soon realize they are expected to conform to accepted standards, someone else's ideas of the proper mode of dress and code of conduct. They are told what to wear, what to read, what to listen to, what to think. Although they are supposed to be free, they still don't have the right to determine the truth for themselves by listening to the Spirit of God or by studying the Word for themselves.

Despite their glowing testimonies and phony smiles, church people are not out to win people to Christ or set people free from bondage nearly as much as they are out to get them onto their roll and into their mold. In religious terms that is called proselytizing, and it is every bit as legalistic as attempting to impose the observance of Jewish law on Gentile believers.

Most of the seven feast days in the Jewish calendar have already been fulfilled by the Lord Jesus Christ; those which are left will be fulfilled when He returns to this earth in glory. The first feast was Passover, the ancient Jewish celebration of the passing of the death angel over the homes of the children of Israel while the firstborn of the Egyptians died. Each Hebrew family took a lamb and slaughtered it, smearing the blood on the doorpost as a sign that they were under God's protection.

Jesus Christ was our Passover Lamb who shed His blood that we might be saved. That's why His crucifixion took place at the time of the Passover Feast. The same religious Jews who were responsible for Christ's crucifixion hurried home from Calvary to partake of the Passover Feast, never realizing they were eyewitnesses to the very event they had been proclaiming by their commemoration.

Next came the weeklong Feast of Unleavened Bread during which time the women were required to thoroughly clean their houses and remove all dust from them because leaven, represented by dust, was a type of sin. Removing all the dust was a sign of the removal of sins by Christ during His three days and nights in the bowels of the earth.

The first Sunday during the Feast of Unleavened Bread was called Firstfruits. In the Jewish tradition this commemorated the bringing of the first and best of the fruits of the harvest to be dedicated to God. It was on the day of Firstfruits that our Lord was resurrected, representing the first and best of a long line of souls who will be raised to new and eternal life because of Him. You and I are part of that huge harvest that is yet to be completed. Fifty days after Passover came the Feast of Pentecost, which was fulfilled when the Holy Spirit was poured out on all believers.

Between Pentecost and the next feast there was an interval of five months. Pentecost was in April; the next feast day, Trumpets, came in October. The interval of five months between the two represents the church age in which you and I are now living. The next feast day to be fulfilled will be that of Trumpets, referring to the fanfare that will mark the triumphant return of our Lord to this earth to begin His millennial reign.

After that comes the Feast of Atonements, looking forward to the day Jesus Christ will cleanse the earth of all sin, remove all sinners from it, and lift the last curse from it. Paul wrote in Romans 8:19 through 23 that this is the moment for which all creation has been groaning and travailing so long, the moment when final atonement will be fulfilled on the earth.

The final feast day to be fulfilled is that of Tabernacles, which was instituted to remind Jews of the time in which God dwelt in a tabernacle with them. Its fulfillment will come when Jesus Christ sets up His kingdom here on earth, inaugurating a thousand-year reign of peace.

There is no need for Gentiles to observe these "times" of the Jewish calendar because those that have not already been fulfilled soon will be. We should know about them and their significance to us as the body of Christ on this earth, but we are not obliged to keep them in their original context because they all point to Christ in whom we are already complete.

"And years" is a reference to the seven seven-year periods of the ancient Jewish calendar, culminating in the fiftieth year, the year of Jubilee. In that year all slaves were set free and all property that had changed hands returned to its original owner. Now we Christians don't need to observe the year of Jubilee; we're living in it. In Luke 4, we read where our Lord went into the synagogue and was handed the scroll to read. Notice the passage He read, and His reason for doing so:

> 18 "The Spirit of the Lord is upon Me,
>   Because He has anointed Me
>   To preach the gospel to the poor;
>   He has sent Me to heal the brokenhearted,
>   To proclaim liberty to the captives
>   And recovery of sight to the blind,
>   To set at liberty those who are oppressed;

19 *To proclaim the acceptable year of the Lord."*

20 Then He closed the book, and gave it back to the attendant and sat down. And the eyes of all who were in the synagogue were fixed on Him. 21 And He began to say to them, "Today this Scripture is fulfilled in your hearing." —Luke 4:18–21

This Scripture has been fulfilled. The "acceptable year of the Lord" has already come. It is here. Jubilee has arrived. The slaves are set free. The property of the just is being returned to its rightful owners. Throughout the land, there is rejoicing and praise to God the Father because He has redeemed us from our oppressors, has opened our blind eyes, has healed our brokenness, and has restored to us our inheritance, just as He promised.

This was just as true in Paul's day. The acceptable year of the Lord had already come before Paul ever set foot in Galatia with the gospel. In fact, that was the good news he brought to these Gentiles. Hearing it had set them free from their bondage. Now here they were turning from that liberty to submit themselves to Jewish law and observance which was only a shadow of what had already taken place by the coming of the Lord Jesus Christ. That's why Paul spoke in such harsh terms to these people. He wanted them to realize how foolish it was to turn their backs on the good news of liberation and surrender to the very law that Christ had come to fulfill in every last detail.

VI. Be as I Am (11–12)

4:11 I am afraid for you, lest I have labored for you in vain.

What is Paul's fear concerning the Galatian believers? Paul is afraid that by their actions they were undoing all the work that he put in on them. He was concerned that they were in danger of destroying the foundation of faith and freedom that he had built during his first visit.

4:12 ¶ Brethren, I urge you to become like me, for I *became* like you. You have not injured me at all.

Paul is telling these people, "Become as I am." What does he mean by this? He means that he began his Christian walk in faith, and he remained in faith. Paul fully understands the message of grace he preached to the

Galatians. He lives by it himself. Now he urges them to remain in God's grace, just as he has done in his own life.

. . . For I am as ye are . . .

Whenever Paul's message of faith is preached now, people tend to say, "Sure, it was easy for Paul to live by faith; he was an apostle, a great man of faith. But it's hard for me to live that way; I'm nobody special."

Realizing these Gentile converts in Galatia might have that attitude, Paul assures them what he is prescribing to them is not impossible. He is saying he lived by faith, and he has confidence they can too because, humanly speaking, he is no different from them. Paul wants the Galatians to understand that of himself he was in no way superior to them. What he can do, they can do too.

It's not our great faith that makes us special; it's God's great grace. That grace is freely available to anyone who will simply receive it. In that sense, Paul has no unique gift. He has the same gift freely offered to everyone: the free gift of God's favor.

. . . You have not injured me at all.

Here Paul is simply saying, "By your actions, you haven't harmed me. I'm just the same as I was." He is implying, "You're not harming me by your actions; it's yourselves who are being injured."

VII. Paul's Infirmity (13–16)

Too many times people take this passage out of context and quoted it as evidence that Paul was a sickly man. In their efforts to discredit the message of healing in the atonement, they link this passage with others from various sources in an attempt to prove Paul's "thorn in the flesh" (2 Corinthians 12:7) was a physical sickness or disease. Sometimes they even go so far as to take this expression about the Galatians being willing to pluck out their own eyes and give them to Paul as an indication that Paul's infirmity was an eye disease. All such teaching is mere speculation. We have no conclusive proof of exactly what it was that Paul was referring to when he spoke of his "thorn in the flesh."

Surely Paul was buffeted in his flesh wherever he went, as we will see. But to interpret Paul's physical hardships and persecutions as an indication that God does not will for His children to be healthy is as much a mistake as interpreting our own children's "hard knocks" in life as evidence we don't will for them to be healthy, prosperous, or successful. Where did we ever get the idea that we humans are better parents than God?

4:13–14 You know that because of physical infirmity I preached the gospel to you at the first.14 And my trial which was in my flesh you did not despise or reject, but you received me as an angel of God, even as Christ Jesus.

Paul spoke here of preaching to the Galatians "through infirmity of the flesh (*NIV*)," but I think a bit of investigation of the Scripture can give us some clue as to what that infirmity might well have been.

Note the last phrase of this verse, "at the first." This tells us *when* Paul came to to preach the gospel to them "through infirmity." It was during his very first missionary trip to Galatia (which we remember is not a city, but a province in which Paul established churches in four cities: *Antioch, Iconium, Derbe,* and *Lystra*). Let's read about this first journey to the province of Galatia, picking up Paul and Barnabas as they leave Antioch:

1 Now it happened in Iconium that they went together to the synagogue of the Jews, and so spoke that a great multitude both of the Jews and of the Greeks believed. 2 But the unbelieving Jews stirred up the Gentiles and poisoned their minds against the brethren. 3 Therefore they stayed there a long time, speaking boldly in the Lord, who was bearing witness to the word of His grace, granting signs and wonders to be done by their hands. 4 But the multitude of the city was divided: part sided with the Jews, and part with the apostles. 5 And when a violent attempt was made by both the Gentiles and Jews, with their rulers, to abuse and stone them, 6 they became aware of it and fled to Lystra and Derbe, cities of Lycaonia, and to the surrounding region. 7 And they were preaching the gospel there. 8 And in Lystra a certain man without strength in his feet was sitting, a cripple from his mother's womb, who had never walked. 9 This man heard Paul speaking. Paul, observing him intently and seeing that he had faith to be healed, 10 said with a loud voice, "Stand up straight on your feet!" And he leaped and walked. —Acts 14:1–10

Paul and Barnabas were quite successful on their first trip to Galatia, but their success was not achieved without opposition. They had to flee from Iconium to Lystra to avoid being stoned by angry crowds the Jews stirred up against them. It was in Lystra that the Holy Spirit, who had granted signs and wonders be done by the hands of Paul and Barnabas, worked another mighty miracle. The lame man, who had been crippled from birth, was healed.

In the healing classic, *Christ the Healer*, we find quite a lengthy discussion of the views of various theologians on the subject of Paul's supposed "weakness of the flesh." One theory advanced was that Paul suffered from a serious eye disease called ophthalmia, a condition marked by constant pain and a continual drainage of water and pus. The person advancing this theory suggested that because of this infectious condition, Paul was a hideous man to look at. He also pointed out the pain caused by this condition would be like that of a stake piercing the eye (hence Paul's reference to a "thorn" in his flesh).

When Paul gazed steadfastly into the eyes of the lame man in Lystra, was there any indication that Paul had difficulty focusing his eyes on the man upon whom he so steadfastly fixed his attention? No. Any mention of Paul's having pain or discomfort in his eyes? No. Does it seem reasonable that this cripple would be moved to great faith for his own physical healing if the man who was preaching the message of healing to him was himself hard to look upon because of his own hideous eye disease? Not likely.

What might have actually been the cause of the infirmity from which Paul suffered during his first stay in Galatia? Notice what happened after this healing took place.

11 Now when the people saw what Paul had done, they raised their voices, saying in the Lycaonian language, "The gods have come down to us in the likeness of men!" 12 And Barnabas they called Zeus, and Paul, Hermes, because he was the chief speaker. 13 Then the priest of Zeus, whose temple was in front of their city, brought oxen and garlands to the gates, intending to sacrifice with the multitudes. 14 But when the apostles Barnabas and Paul heard this, they tore their clothes and ran in among the multitude, crying out 15 and saying, "Men, why are you doing these things? We also are men with the same nature as you, and preach to you that you should turn from these useless things to

the living God, who made the heaven, the earth, the sea, and all things that are in them, 16 who in bygone generations allowed all nations to walk in their own ways. 17 Nevertheless He did not leave Himself without witness, in that He did good, gave us rain from heaven and fruitful seasons, filling our hearts with food and gladness." 18 And with these sayings they could scarcely restrain the multitudes from sacrificing to them. —Acts 14:11–18

As a result of the healing of the lame man, the people of Lystra were convinced Paul and Barnabas were Greek gods in the form of men. Notice what Paul told them in verse 15: "Sirs, why do ye these things? We also are men of like passions with you." That reminds us of his words in Galatians 4:12, "I beseech you, be as I am; for I am as ye are." Why did these people want to worship Paul and Barnabas? Because the Holy Spirit had performed miracles through them, so the people looked upon them as gods.

Note again in Galatians 4:14 what Paul says about the way he had been received when he first brought the gospel to Galatia: "And my temptation which was in my flesh ye despised not, nor rejected; but received me as an angel of God, even as Christ Jesus." Paul reminds the Galatians that when he first brought them the gospel of grace, they had received him as if he were Jesus Christ Himself.

Paul and Barnabas had to talk fast and hard to persuade the people of Lystra they were not Greek gods in human flesh, but were representatives of the one true God, creator of heaven and earth. All this commotion in Lystra attracted the attention of the Jews. The following passage describes what happened next:

19 Then Jews from Antioch and Iconium came there; and having persuaded the multitudes, they stoned Paul and dragged him out of the city, supposing him to be dead. 20 However, when the disciples gathered around him, he rose up and went into the city. And the next day he departed with Barnabas to Derbe. 21 And when they had preached the gospel to that city and made many disciples, they returned to Lystra, Iconium, and Antioch, 22 strengthening the souls of the disciples, exhorting them to continue in the faith, and saying, "We must through many tribulations enter the kingdom of God." 23 So when they had appointed elders in every church, and prayed with fasting, they commended

them to the Lord in whom they had believed. —Acts 14:19–23

Paul was stoned by the Jews in Lystra. Most biblical scholars agree Paul was actually dead, but was restored to life by God. Some even go so far as to speculate that this might have been the time during which he was taken up into the third heaven where he saw unspeakable things (2 Corinthians 12). Whether this is so or not, Paul was assumed dead by the crowds who dragged him out of the city where they discarded what they thought to be his dead body. As the disciples stood around his prostrate form, Paul was revived, got to his feet and immediately went right back into the city. From there, he and Barnabas continued their missionary journey, retracing their steps throughout the whole province of Galatia, visiting the cities of Derbe, Iconium, and Antioch, besides returning to visit Lystra.

What do you think might have been Paul's appearance and physical condition after having just been stoned and dragged out of the city of Lystra? Is it likely he showed any signs in his body of the beating he had just experienced? I'm sure he did. He was probably black and blue all over. His reference to the Galatians having been willing to have plucked out their own eyes for his sake could be an indication his own eyes were temporarily damaged, perhaps black or even swollen shut, as he and Barnabas made their way through the cities of Galatia.

In any case, I believe there is much stronger evidence that the infirmity through which Paul preached while in Galatia was a temporary, man-induced condition he eventually overcame, rather than being some chronic debilitating physical disease that he had to live with all his life.

. . . And my temptation which was in my flesh ye despised not, nor rejected; but received me as an angel of God, even as Christ Jesus.

The expression "my temptation" actually means my test. Paul was simply saying here, "When I came to you the first time, I was suffering from the test of faith I had just endured, but you did not let my repulsive physical condition deter you from receiving me as you would have received the Lord Himself."

4:15 ¶ What then was the blessing you *enjoyed*? For I bear you witness that, if possible, you would have plucked out your own eyes and given them to me.

It's as if Paul is saying, "Since you were so gracious to receive me as a messenger of God, why have you now rejected the message I brought you to turn to a different messenger with a different message? My message is the same. You loved me at first and hate me now. I have not changed, but you have. Then, you were in such sympathy with my physical pain and suffering, if you could have, you would have given your own eyes (your right arm) to be a help to me."

4:16 Have I therefore become your enemy because I tell you the truth?

"What has happened to change that spirit of loving brotherhood we shared? What have I done to betray you so that now you no longer trust me? All I have ever done is what I did when I first came to you (tell the truth). For that have I now become your enemy?"

4:17–31 Sarah and Hagar

I. Paul's Concern for the Galatians (17–20)

4:17 ¶ They zealously court you, *but* for no good; yes, they want to exclude you, that you may be zealous for them.

They zealously affect you, but not well. . .

"They" refers to the legalistic Judaizers. The Greek word translated "affect" is *zeloo*, from which we derive our English word *zealous*. According to *Strong's Concordance*, this word means "to have warmth of feeling for or against" someone or something. So this verse could be paraphrased: "These legalistic Judaizers are eager to court you, but their intentions are not honorable."

. . . Yea, they would exclude you, that ye might affect them.

Paul is telling them, "They are trying to woo you away from us in order to win your affection for themselves." Paul likens the Judaizers to adulterers who try to seduce people from their mates and into an extramarital affair. He is trying to warn the Galatians not to be misled by the feigned ardor and enticing words of these clever Jews because their ultimate motive is selfish: they just want to destroy the relationship the Galatian believers had with the Lord.

4:18 But it is good to be zealous in a good thing always, and not only when I am present with you.

Paul is telling the Galatians it is fine to be courted by someone when that person's intentions are good. Paul wants someone to court them who preaches his same message. But, now that he was far away from them, he warns them about being led astray from their covenant relationship by unfaithful seducers.

4:19 My little children, for whom I labor in birth again until Christ is formed in you,

Here it would seem that Paul is addressing these Galatians as though they are unbelievers, saying that he is "travailing" (praying strongly) to bring them to new birth. That is not what he meant. These are believers; they have already been born again, but they have turned away from the Word of God and slipped into legalistic works. Paul's travail here refers to his intercessory prayer for them. The first time Paul went through travail for the Galatians, it was to bring them to the new birth. Now that they are in the kingdom of God, he wants them to know his labor for them has not ended. He continues to pray for them, that their nature will be conformed to the image of the Christ who lives within them in the person of the Holy Spirit.

That should be a lesson for us today. Just because people have been born again does not mean we no longer need to pray for them. Once they are reborn, they are still just babes in Christ, like these Galatians. They still need to be formed, shaped, and developed. They need us to pray for them through our intercession.

Even mature believers and established churches need prayer support. Paul said he prayed for the Ephesians "after I heard of your faith in the Lord Jesus, and love unto all the saints" (Ephesains 1:15). He did the same for the Colossians (Colossians 1:3–4). None of us are so fully developed, so mature in the Lord, that we don't still need the support of other believers to overcome the trials, temptations, and obstacles our enemy throws up in front of us to discourage and destroy us. In the church we should be praying together with our brothers and sisters in Christ, pulling together, strengthening and encouraging one another, bearing each other's burdens, forgiving each other, lifting up the weak and the fallen, drawing hope and encouragement from each other, and edifying each other, "till we all come in the unity of the faith, and of the knowledge of the Son of God, unto a perfect man, unto the measure of the stature of the fulness of Christ" (Ephesians 4:13).

4:20 I would like to be present with you now and to change my tone; for I have doubts about you.

In this letter Paul is not dealing gently with these people. He has to be harsh with them. He has to rebuke them for their foolishness and error. He has to verbally correct them, even going so far as to call them "Galatian idiots" (*Phillips Translation*). Now he makes it clear he doesn't like to speak to them in that tone of voice. The only reason he does is so was because he has real doubts about their commitment.

The *New International Version* captures Paul's mood here when it translates Galatians 4:17 through 20 in these words:

> 17 Those people are zealous to win you over, but for no good. What they want is to alienate you from us, so that you may have zeal for them. 18 It is fine to be zealous, provided the purpose is good, and to be so always, not just when I am with you. 19 My dear children, for whom I am again in the pains of childbirth until Christ is formed in you, 20 how I wish I could be with you now and change my tone, because I am perplexed about you!

II. Abraham's Two Sons (21–23)

4:21 ¶ Tell me, you who desire to be under the law, do you not hear the law?

The Greek word translated "hear" actually means understand. In verse 21, Paul begins to introduce chapter 5 in which he emphasizes two themes: freedom in Christ and life by the Spirit. He begins his introduction to these themes by asking the Galatians a puzzling question: "You who want to be under the law, don't you understand the law?"

This seems a strange question for Paul to ask people he has been reproving for three and a half chapters about the law. Doesn't he realize these people had to know about the law in order to keep it? Yes, he does. He also knows there is a difference between knowing the law or knowing *about* the law and fully understanding the law. It's possible to have knowledge of something and still never understand the meaning of it.

For example, how many orthodox Jews today fully understand the law they are so careful to observe? How many of them realize everything in it, every ritual and ceremony and requirement of it, points to Jesus Christ? They know the letter of the law, but they really don't know what the letter symbolizes. They see the law well, but they are not able to look beyond it to see the one to whom it points.

That's nothing new. It was true of the Jews in Jesus' day. Do you remember what He told the Pharisees who questioned His authority? "You search the Scriptures because you think that in them you have eternal life: but the Scriptures point to Me" (John 5:39). The scribes and Pharisees knew the law perfectly. They kept it in minute detail. Yet they missed the whole point of it.

The law could not save them; it only pointed to Jesus. When He stood before them in flesh and blood, they refused to recognize and acknowledge Him. They held to the letter of the law and rejected the living fulfillment of the law. That was not only foolish, it was also tragic. Because of their misguided zeal, the Pharisees missed the very salvation they were so desperately seeking. That's the message Paul tries to get across to these foolish Galatians who have turned their backs on the door and went back to the signpost.

> **4:22–23 For it is written that Abraham had two sons: the one by a bondwoman, the other by a freewoman. 23 But he *who was* of the bondwoman was born according to the flesh, and he of the freewoman through promise,**

Here Paul unfolds to these spiritually blind Galatians what the law was all about. To explain the law and its purpose, he went all the way back to the time of Abraham. He had lived 430 years before the law ever came into existence. He uses the two sons of Abraham as examples of law and grace, and the works of the flesh and the fruit of the Spirit. We will look at these in more detail as we follow Paul's logic through a comparison of the offspring of the bondmaid and the offspring of the free woman.

III. Sarah and Hagar (24–27)

> **4:24 which things are symbolic. For these are the two covenants: the one from Mount Sinai which gives birth to bondage, which is Hagar—**

Which things are an allegory. . . .

When Paul says the two offspring of Abraham are an "allegory," he meant they are an analogy. They represent something beyond themselves.

We know this is true, because Abraham himself represented something far more universal and everlasting than he ever imagined in his own lifetime. In this context, Abraham is a type of the individual believer. The two women living in his tent with him are a type of the two messages to which the believer is exposed and is free to devote himself. The free woman, Sarah, symbolizes grace or the promise of God. The bondmaid, Hagar, symbolizes the law. In the story of the relationship between these three Old Testament figures and their offspring, we see portrayed symbolically the whole conflict between the law and grace.

By faith in Christ, the Seed of Abraham, you and I became participants in the Abrahamic covenant with the patriarch of old. Therefore, the things that affected him still affect us today because he represents us. Although the law did not technically come into existence until "430 years later"(3:17), Abraham had a type of the law right there in his tent. Her name was Hagar. He also had a type of grace living in his tent. She was called Sarah. From which of these two are you and I descended? To answer that question, let's consider each of these two women separately.

First, what was Hagar's position in the family? She was a bondmaid, a slave. What was her country of origin; where did she come from? She was an Egyptian. Think about that for a moment. What was Egypt a type of in the Old Testament? Egypt always represented exile and bondage, our life as unbelievers.

Before you and I were converted, we were living in a spiritual Egypt. We were exiled from our loving heavenly Father, held in bondage, slaves to sin. But then there came a day when we crossed the Red Sea, a type of the blood of the Lord Jesus Christ, and we walked out of bondage into liberty. Our enemies were cut off from us, washed away by the blood of Jesus. We walked away free men.

As we traveled, we had to do some growing up. We developed and matured spiritually. Following the Lord, we crossed the Jordan and entered into our promised land of the life of faith.

Even though we were set free when we left Egypt, we brought a part of it with us. Like Abraham, we had with us in our tent (body) not only our Sarah of grace, but our Hagar of the law. Our Hagar, our Egyptian, was the flesh. Although we were redeemed by grace, born again of the Spirit, we still have not rid ourselves of the flesh. That is something with which we must contend as long as our regenerated spirit is in this body of flesh. One day, we will be released from this earthly, natural body and caught up to heaven where we will live forever in perfect freedom and holiness. Until that day, you and I must dominate the flesh by the spirit.

New Testament writers like Paul understood this principle. That's why they wrote things like, "For I know that in me (that is, in my flesh) dwelleth no good thing" (Romans 7:18). That is not to say that we are to hate our flesh, to abhor, neglect, or punish it through asceticism. It just means we are to take authority and dominion over our fleshly lusts and not allow them to dictate to us. I like the answer Smith Wigglesworth gave one day when someone asked him if he ever felt bad: "I never ask myself how I feel," he replied quickly, "I tell myself how I feel!" As free men, that's the way we are to live in relation to our Egyptian bond slave. We are to exercise dominion over it, making it conform to our desires and wishes rather than the other way around.

We will always have the flesh to contend with in this life, but the flesh is not our wife. Our wife is Sarah, the type of the inward man, the regenerated spirit, the new creation. We are to live with her in harmony and peace. We are to become one in union with her.

In the case of Abraham, although he was promised offspring through Sarah (representing the spirit), he became impatient and took unto himself Hagar (representing the flesh). As a result of that union, Hagar gave birth to a son named Ishmael. Later on, Abraham did father a child through Sarah whom they called Isaac. Consequently, two sets of offspring were produced by Abraham: those of the flesh (through Ishmael, a type of the works of the flesh) and those of the spirit (through Isaac, a type of the fruit of the spirit).

Like our father Abraham, we have a choice of which of these two "women" we will unite ourselves with. We have two voices calling out to us for our attention, seeking our commitment. One voice is that of the flesh; the other is that of the spirit. We must decide which we will give ear to, which one we will "mind." Paul told us that "to be carnally minded is death; but to be spiritually minded is life and peace" (Romans 8:6). Notice, both of these states of mind produce something; one produces death, the other produces life and peace. Thus, our choice of mates will determine the offspring or fruit produced in our lives.

The fruit of our union does not end with the first generation. It has the ability to go on reproducing itself indefinitely. The fruit Abraham produced through Hagar and Sarah kept on multiplying itself. Ishmael produced only a natural race, the Arabs. Isaac produced a natural race, the Jews, which was also a spiritual race, the redeemed. One is temporal; the other is eternal. One lasts for a space of a few hundred earth years; the other endures forever and ever. One is illegitimate (because there is no true marriage to the law); the other is legitimate (a product of the marriage of the human spirit with God's Spirit). One produces death; the other produces life and peace.

A. The Two Sons

. . . For these are the two covenants; the one from the mount Sinai, which gendereth to bondage, which is Agar."

Hagar represents the old covenant that was handed down to Moses on Mount Sinai, which is in Arabia. The law was not given in the promised land of Israel; it originated in Arabia, in the land of cursing. That is an important point.

> **4:25 for this Hagar is Mount Sinai in Arabia, and corresponds to Jerusalem which now is, and is in bondage with her children—**

The first covenant, the old covenant symbolized by Hagar, corresponds to the Jewish nation centered in ancient Jerusalem, which was in bondage both literally and figuratively at the time Paul writes these words. Literally, the city of Jerusalem is under the yoke of Rome. Spiritually, it is under the yoke of the law. "With her children" is a reference to the two sets of offspring fathered by Abraham: 1) a natural race, the Jews, who were and are in bondage to the law; and 2) a spiritual race, the church of Jesus Christ, which is free. This second race is the true Israel, as we read in the ninth chapter of Romans:

> 6 But it is not that the word of God has taken no effect. For they are not all Israel who are of Israel, 7 nor are they all children because they are the seed of Abraham; but, "In Isaac your seed shall be called." 8 That is, those who are the children of the flesh, these are not the children of God; but the children of the promise are counted as the seed. 9 For this is the word of promise: "At this time I will come and Sarah shall have a son." 10 And not only this, but when Rebecca also had conceived by one man, even by our father Isaac 11 (for the children not yet being born, nor having done any good or evil, that the purpose of God according to election might stand, not of works but of Him who calls), 12 it was said to her, "The older shall serve the younger." 13 As it is written, "Jacob I have loved, but Esau I have hated." —Romans 9:6–13

Now God did not hate Esau and love Jacob for no reason, as we saw previously. Even before they were born, God looked ahead into their lives.

Through foreknowledge, He was aware of the faith resident in Jacob and the unbelief that would motivate Esau. God did not hate Esau personally; He hated the unbelief he stood for. Likewise, God didn't love Jacob as much personally (certainly not his human nature and actions) as He loved the faith he represented.

When Paul spoke of the two offspring of Isaac, he was doing more than examining their personal lives. He was using the two to symbolize the two types of people in the world: 1) those, like Esau, who doubt and dis-believe, and 2) those like Jacob, who though far from perfect, humanly speaking are yet counted righteous by God because of their faith in Him.

This same analogy applies in the case of Ishmael and Isaac. They represent two totally different heritages. One was a product of the flesh, the result of human planning, the fruit of man, a child of the law. The other was a product of the spirit, the result of divine planning, the fruit of the Holy Spirit, a child of the promise. In other words, Ishmael was Abraham's idea; Isaac was God's idea. That's why Ishmael, the natural child, had no part in the inheritance of Isaac, the spiritual child. This is what Paul is referring to when he says that not all of Israel (the natural seed of Abraham) is part of the true Israel (the spiritual seed of Abraham).

B. The Two Mountains

4:26 but the Jerusalem above is free, which is the mother of us all.

In verses 24 and 25, Mount Sinai represents the giving of the law. Because it came to be identified with those who held to the law and rejected the risen Christ, the promised Messiah, it came to be a type of the rejection of the promises of God. As such, Mount Sinai symbolizes legalism, which is bondage.

According to Paul, the Old Jerusalem, the Jerusalem of the natural Jews, is an example of the bondage in which those people live who look to the law for their justification. Since justification comes not by works of the law, but by faith in the promises (the integrity) of God, the true Israel is made up of all those who look to Him for their redemption. Their holy city then is not an earthly habitation built by the hands of men; it is the New Jerusalem, "which is above" (cf. Hebrews 11:10).

Paul says this New Jerusalem is "the mother of us all." "The mother" is a reference to the new birth. "Us all" refers to all who have been born again, not of the flesh but of the Spirit. The center of Jerusalem is Mount

Zion. It is to this mount Israel looks for its deliverance. But the true Mount Zion, like the true Jerusalem, is not a natural, physical place; it's a spiritual one. Just as Mount Sinai corresponds to the Old Jerusalem, the earthly Jerusalem, Mount Zion corresponds to the New Jerusalem, the heavenly Jerusalem.

The writer of Hebrews tells us:

> 18 For you have not come to the mountain that may be touched and that burned with fire, and to blackness and darkness and tempest, 19 and the sound of a trumpet and the voice of words, so that those who heard it begged that the word should not be spoken to them anymore. 20 (For they could not endure what was commanded: "And if so much as a beast touches the mountain, it shall be stoned or shot with an arrow." 21 And so terrifying was the sight that Moses said, "I am exceedingly afraid and trembling.") 22 But you have come to Mount Zion and to the city of the living God, the heavenly Jerusalem, to an innumerable company of angels, 23 to the general assembly and church of the firstborn who are registered in heaven, to God the Judge of all, to the spirits of just men made perfect, 24 to Jesus the Mediator of the new covenant, and to the blood of sprinkling that speaks better things than that of Abel. —Hebrews 12:18–24

What mountain did Moses stand before in the midst of thunder and lightning and darkness? Mount Sinai, where the law was given. But you and I have not come to that mountain. As this passage points out, we have come to Mount Zion "and unto the city of the living God, the heavenly Jerusalem" (v. 22). We came to that mountain when we "married Sarah," when we joined ourselves in union with God through faith in His promises. Faith always connects a person to the promises.

At Mount Zion, we became a part of "the general assembly and church of the firstborn," those whose names are "written in heaven." We became one with "God the Judge of all." We found our home in the "company of angels" and with the "just men made perfect." Who are these "just men made perfect"? All those who have come to God through faith, "being justified freely by his grace through the redemption that is in Christ Jesus" (Romans 3:24).

C. The Two Nations

4:27 For it is written:

> *"Rejoice, O barren,*
> *You who do not bear!*
> *Break forth and shout,*
> *You who are not in labor!*
> *For the desolate has many more children*
> *Than she who has a husband."*

This verse refers to Isaiah 54:1, "Sing, O barren, thou that didst not bear; break forth into singing, and cry aloud, thou that didst not travail with child: for more are the children of the desolate than the children of the married wife, saith the LORD."

Rejoice, thou barren that bearest not; break forth and cry, thou that travailest not. . . .

The barren one here refers to Sarah. She was told of the Lord to break forth into singing and rejoicing. When? Before she had even yet become pregnant. Why was she to be so joyful when she was still barren?

. . . For the desolate hath many more children than she which hath an husband.

Sarah was told to rejoice because of the promise of the Lord. Her joy was not to be based on what she saw with her eyes, but on what she heard from God.

Does that remind you of a scripture? "So then faith cometh by hearing, and hearing by the word of God" (Romans 10:17). Faith does not wait for the physical manifestation before it finds expression; it rejoices upon hearing from God. Why? Faith knows that what God promises He provides. Nothing in all the world is as sure as a promise from God, provided we, like Abraham, are "fully persuaded that, what he [has] promised, he [is] able also to perform" (Romans 4:21). For that kind of assurance we receive not only the manifestation of what was promised, but we also receive something far greater, the righteousness of God: "And therefore it was imputed to him for righteousness" (v. 22).

The faith life is a double blessing. When we believe God, we freely receive what we have been promised; then, in addition, God rewards our faith by calling us righteous. In other words, God does all the work, all the giving; all we do is believe Him. Yet we get both the promised blessing and a reward — as though we had done the giving! This is what justification means to the individual believer: "All I did was believe God, and I received a blessing and a reward, just as if I'd done the work."

Notice again when this belief, this rejoicing, is to take place: before the physical manifestation. Do you recall what Jesus told His disciples about how to get their prayers answered? "Therefore I say unto you, What things soever ye desire, when ye pray, believe that ye receive them, and ye shall have them" (Mark 11:24). "When ye pray, believe." The key to answered prayer is to believe at the time of the prayer. In essence, that's what Abraham did. He believed when he heard the Word of God, not when he saw the manifestation of what was promised him. For that, he received the double blessing of manifestation and righteousness.

"The desolate" in Galatians 4:27 refers to righteous Sarah who, though she was barren, rejoiced at the promise of God that she would one day produce more offspring than the one in her household who had already given birth to a son. The offspring of Hagar, the bondmaid, would go on to produce a long line of earthly descendants who would multiply and cover the earth. We call the people of that physical nation Arabs. Sarah produced two nations through her offspring, a spiritual race of believers and the natural nation of Israel. The difference is the offspring of Sarah would last not only for the short span we call time, but, being spiritual, would endure throughout all eternity.

There is a lesson here. What we do in the natural, physical realm is important because by our actions we plant seeds that will produce a harvest either of good or of evil long after we are gone.How much more important is it that we give attention to our spiritual sowing because it has eternal significance. The fruit produced by that seed will never die.

IV. The Children of Promise (28–31)

4:28 ¶ Now we, brethren, as Isaac was, are children of promise.

But most of us are not Jews. That doesn't matter. The children of promise include all nations around the world (Genesis 12:3). Anyone who has received the Lord Jesus Christ as his personal Savior has entered into the

Abrahamic covenant and has become the seed of Abraham. Abraham's seed is not determined by flesh, but is counted by spirit, according to the promise. We become heirs of the promise with Isaac.

4:29 But, as he who was born according to the flesh then persecuted him *who was born* according to the Spirit, even so it is now.

Here Paul is referring to the fact that Isaac, the son of promise, the son born after the Spirit of God, was persecuted by Ishmael, the natural son, the son born after the flesh. He is saying those who were born of God have always been the object of scorn, ridicule, and abuse by those who were born only of the flesh. This was especially true in the day in which Paul wrote these words, since the Christian church was hounded and persecuted not only by the paganistic Romans, but especially by the legalistic Jews.

4:30 Nevertheless what does the Scripture say? *"Cast out the bondwoman and her son, for the son of the bondwoman shall not be heir with the son of the freewoman."*

Genesis 21 gives us an idea of how it happened:

9 And Sarah saw the son of Hagar the Egyptian, whom she had borne to Abraham, scoffing. 10 Therefore she said to Abraham, "Cast out this bondwoman and her son; for the son of this bondwoman shall not be heir with my son, namely with Isaac." 11 And the matter was very displeasing in Abraham's sight because of his son. 12 But God said to Abraham, "Do not let it be displeasing in your sight because of the lad or because of your bondwoman. Whatever Sarah has said to you, listen to her voice; for in Isaac your seed shall be called. 13 Yet I will also make a nation of the son of the bondwoman, because he is your seed. 14 So Abraham rose early in the morning, and took bread and a skin of water; and putting it on her shoulder, he gave it and the boy to Hagar, and sent her away. Then she departed and wandered in the Wilderness of Beersheba. —21:9–14

Sarah realized that she had made a mistake in offering her handmaid to Abraham to bear him the child (Genesis 16:1–16). Finally she warned

Abraham to get rid of Hagar and her son because Ishmael could not be allowed to have any part in the inheritance that rightfully belonged to Isaac, the child of promise. Being a just and honest man, Abraham was reluctant to cast out Hagar and Ishmael, because the boy was his son just as Isaac was. However, the Lord commanded Abraham to do as Sarah had said, noting that it would be through Isaac alone that the covenant would be fulfilled. In obedience to God, Abraham sent Hagar and Ishmael away.

Abraham's feelings reflect our own. Many times we are hesitant to put away the seed of our carnal nature to give total place to the seed of our spiritual nature. We want to hang on to our fleshly nature because it, too, seems to be a vital part of us. Yet God knows that nothing must come between us and Him; nothing must be allowed to keep us from devoting our full attention and devotion to the things of the spirit.

Abraham was ordered not only to get rid of Ishmael but also Hagar. So many times we want to try to rid ourselves of the product of our flesh, but still pet and excuse the flesh itself. In Galatians 5:24 we will see where Paul said that those who "are Christ's have crucified the flesh with the affections and lusts" of it. It is not only the flesh we must subdue, but also its affections and desires. Not only did Hagar have to depart, her seed also had to depart with her.

In Colossians 3:9 and 10, we read these words: "Lie not one to another, seeing that ye have put off the old man with his deeds; and have put on the new man, which is renewed in knowledge after the image of him that created him." In this case, the "old man" is Hagar and the "deeds" are Ishmael. Notice, we are not to rid ourselves of Hagar and keep Ishmael, nor are we to rid ourselves of Ishmael and keep Hagar. We are to put off both the old man and his nature and put on the new man. The old man"is a reference to our flesh. We are to put it back on the level of a slave, exercising authority and dominion over it, not allowing it to dictate or lord over us.

When Paul spoke of crucifying the flesh, he did not mean we have to kill our old nature every day. Our old man was put to death at the cross. He is dead, and the life we now live in the flesh, we live by the faith of the Son of God who loved us and gave Himself for us (Galatians 2:20). Even though our old man, our flesh, is dead in God's sight, we need to count it dead in our own lives. We need to see it as God sees it. We have to dominate it by operating in the power of the Spirit.

4:31 So then, brethren, we are not children of the bondwoman but of the free.

You and I are the product of the faith of Abraham. We who are of faith are blessed with believing Abraham. We are the seed of Abraham. We are heirs according to the promise. We are the children of the promise. We have been set free from the curse of the law to live in the blessing of Abraham.

5:1–18 Circumcision

I. Stand Fast in Liberty (1)

In the last chapter we saw that both Ishmael and Isaac were offspring of Abraham, yet each represents a totally different approach to God. Ishmael, the child of the flesh, represents works of the flesh; Isaac, the child of the promise, represents the grace of God. The two lived for a time in the same household, growing up together in their father's home. But there came a time when the child of flesh was cast out in order to give way to the child of promise. This, we saw, is an illustration of the law and the Abrahamic covenant.

Just as Isaac was promised to Abraham and Sarah before the birth of Ishmael, so the covenant God made with Abraham was given before the law came on the scene. After the birth of Ishmael (representing the giving of the law), the promise of the son was fulfilled; Isaac was born. This is a symbolic representation of the fulfillment of the Abrahamic covenant. For a time the two existed together, but the child of the flesh (the child of the bondwoman) never had a part in the inheritance of the child of promise (the child of the freewoman). That's why eventually the illegitimate son (the law) had to go to give place to the true son and heir of Abraham (the product of faith), the one who came not by natural means but by the promise and power of God.

By this allegory, Paul shows the Galatians they were not the offspring of the illegitimate son, the law, but were the offspring of the legitimate son, the one given by the grace of God and received by faith. As such, they haveno part in the law, and the law had no part in them. In Christ Jesus they had been set free from the law of sin and death that they might freely live unto righteousness and peace.

5:1 ¶ Stand fast therefore in the liberty by which Christ has made us free, and do not be entangled again with a yoke of bondage.

This expression "stand fast" was a military term meaning "to hold one's ground." Paul is telling these people that once they have gained ground in their spiritual life, they are to hold fast to it and not allow the enemy to wrest it from them.

Liberty is freedom, but freedom is not free. It doesn't come easy. Nor does a person remain free without effort. Just as it takes courage and commitment to hold on to political freedom, so it requires dedicated effort to preserve spiritual liberty. As citizens of the kingdom of God, we must be every bit as vigilant to preserve and protect our spiritual freedom as we must be as citizens of the United States in preserving and protecting our political freedom. In both cases we have an enemy who will destroy and enslave us if we are not continually on our guard.

Paul is warning these people that now that they are free, they have to stand firm in that freedom lest it be taken away from them by their enemy. But notice he tells them to stand fast "in the liberty wherewith Christ hath made us free." Paul knows we must be aware of both the enemy without and the enemy within. He also knows often those we must guard ourselves against most are not those who come against us openly, but those in our own midst who would like to see us yield to their authority and viewpoint. In other words, Paul warns against religion, the manmade system of rules and regulations that gives an appearance of godliness and devotion by its imposed restraints but which has no real power to bless and heal and set free.

. . . And be not entangled again with the yoke of bondage . . .

Paul urges the Galatian believers not to allow anyone to put them back into slavery to man-imposed laws, which he calls bondage. He wants the believers in Galatia to be free, totally free. That includes freedom from religion as much as freedom from sin.

Wherever I preach this message of liberty in Christ, someone always accuses me of "giving people a license to sin." It seems so hard for some people to accept true liberty, either for themselves or for others. They view freedom from the stranglehold of religion as some sort of spiritual anarchy in which people are just turned loose to commit all the pent-up sins that have been held in check by rules and regulations. That is a false concept of Christian righteousness and responsibility.

If God's own children cannot be set free to think, speak, and act as they choose, if they must be kept chained by a system of do's and don'ts, then the new birth is no better than the life of sin. In that case, God simply took us out of one bondage into another. Grace is not a license to sin; it is a license to serve. God gives us freedom to serve Him and binds us only with love.

Churches that preach rules and regulations eventually dry up from within, because God is not a dictator; He's a liberator. Jesus said He came to do the will of His Father in heaven; to loose bonds, to free captives, to set at liberty them that are bruised. It is Satan who binds, not God. Our Father wants us to be free. That means free to worship and love and serve Him as we will, not as we are forced to do. That's why the message of freedom always attracts crowds. People want to be free, not to sin, but to live. They don't come to church to hear the message of grace and love so they can go out and sin all they want to. They come to hear it so they can go out and enjoy the abundant life their savior bled and died to purchase for them.

The only people who are afraid to set the church free are those who don't trust it. The reason they don't trust others with freedom is because they don't trust themselves. They are the very ones who need to be set free from their own self-imposed legalism. Once they are free, they can allow the church to be liberated so it can go and liberate others. That's God's plan as revealed in the book of Galatians.

II. Circumcision or Christ? (2–6)

The big issue in Galatia at this time is circumcision, which is part of the Mosaic law, part of the old covenant. Even in the day in which it was instituted, it was never meant to provide salvation, because the law itself was not given as a means of salvation but only to reveal to man his need of a savior. Circumcision was an outward physical sign of the covenant between God and Abraham. Circumcision didn't save Abraham; it was simply intended to symbolize outwardly what had happened to him inwardly.

Like the law of which it was a part, circumcision was only a sign to the Jews to teach them about faith. In a way, it was the Old Testament equivalent of the New Testament practice of water baptism. Baptism is an outward sign of an inward occurrence. It presents in symbolic language the spiritual truth of a person being dead, buried, and raised to new life in Christ. Down through the years this practice has lost some of its significance because some segments of the church have misinterpreted it. They have taken the outward sign of salvation and made it the means of salvation, which is a mistake. Water baptism does not save; it only tells the world that salvation has taken place in a person's life. To substitute the physical symbol for the spiritual reality is to miss the reality.

This is what had happened through the years since the practice of circumcision had been given by God to Abraham as a sign of his covenant relationship with the Lord. Now it is necessary for Paul to write to Gentiles to explain that by depending on a physical symbol of an old covenant rela-tionship, they are actually depriving themselves of the spiritual reality the symbol represented.

5:2 Indeed I, Paul, say to you that if you become circumcised, Christ will profit you nothing.

Circumcision has natural benefits, but no real spiritual benefits. If a per-son allows himself to be circumcised thinking by doing so he is achieving salvation, then Christ can be of no value to him. How can that man be saved by grace through faith in the finished work of Jesus on the cross if he is trusting a physical sign of the law in his own body? His faith in his own shed blood would be keeping him from true faith in the shed blood of Jesus Christ.

5:3 And I testify again to every man who becomes circumcised that he is a debtor to keep the whole law.

Again Paul is speaking here of circumcision for spiritual reasons. In verse 2, he refers to circumcision as an attempt to obtain salvation and in verse 3, of circumcision as an attempt to attain spirituality. Paul explains if a person thinks he should be circumcised to keep the law, to be "holy," then logi-cally he should not stop at circumcision; he should keep the whole of the Jewish law. If keeping the law makes a person "holy," then he is obligated to keep all the law to be completely holy. He can't just pick and choose some parts and neglect others; he is obliged to keep every tiny detail of it. Once he begins in the law, even the most minor aspects, he is obligated, a debtor, to keep the whole law.

In our day, there are those who are so legalistic in their thinking they believe they should go back and keep the Jewish Sabbath. Consequently, Saturday becomes their day of rest and worship, which is fine. However, Paul points out if they really believe they should keep the law, they ought to keep the whole law, not just one minor requirement of it. To be consis-tent, such people ought to build a temple in accordance with the instruc-tions given by God in the Old Testament, anoint priests and Levites, dress them in the robes and turbans of ancient Israel, bring in grain and meal and drink offerings to the Lord, offer up burnt animal sacrifices, and do everything else required by Jewish law because the law stipulates that to violate one part is to violate it all.

James 2:10 says, "For whosoever shall keep the whole law, and yet offend in one point, he is guilty of all." Paul explains to the Galatians: "If you keep one part of the law, the part about circumcision, then you're obliged to keep the entire law." That would put the Gentile Galatians in the position of keeping a system of laws and regulations they know virtually nothing about because they had never been subject to it. Paul wants them to see how blessed and free they are in Christ Jesus who fulfilled all those minute details for them once and for all.

5:4 You have become estranged from Christ, you who *attempt to* be justified by law; you have fallen from grace.

When Paul speaks here of being "justified," he is referring to the new birth experience. He explains that anyone trying to be born again by keeping the law is destined to failure because the New Birth does not come by the law, but by grace through faith.

Another way to look at it is this: If anyone thinks he can be saved by the righteousness he achieves in keeping the law, he is doomed because no one has ever kept the law perfectly. Even if he could keep it to perfection, he would still be doomed, because no flesh will be justified by works of the law. Therefore, to trust in the law for salvation is to deny the only real means of salvation offered to man, redemption through the grace of God by faith in His Son Jesus Christ.

Jesus had said that no one could come to the Father except by Him (John 14:6). To try to get to God through the law is to try to reach Him other than by Jesus, and there is no other way. That's what Paul means when he says-such people have fallen from grace. He means as long as they are trying to win salvation, they will never have it, because it can be received only as a free gift of God's grace. If a person insists on winning it by his own efforts, he will never have it. Those self-efforts include water baptism, church membership, good works, acts of penance, or anything other than simple faith in the finished work of Jesus Christ on the cross of Calvary.

5:5 For we through the Spirit eagerly wait for the hope of righteousness by faith.

One of the fruits of the Spirit is patience. Patience always looks forward to the hope of righteousness that lies ahead. Many times it may look as though it would be easier to have our needs met by some works of the law rather than by simply trusting God, but this is usually evidence of a lack of patience. We get tired of waiting on the Lord so we jump up and take some action on our own, which is usually a mistake that ends up costing us more than if we had simply exercised faith a little while longer. Paul was telling the Galatians to be patient; their righteousness would be revealed, not by their attempts at self-righteousness, but through faith in the Lord who imputes righteousness.

5:6 For in Christ Jesus neither circumcision nor uncircumcision avails anything, but faith working through love.

Circumcision is done on the outward man, but faith is an action of the inner man. Man looks on the outward appearance, but God looks on the inside. Faith pleases God, not an outward work like circumcision. Whether a person is circumcised or not circumcised is of no significance to God; it avails nothing. What matters to God is faith that manifests itself in love, love for God and love for our fellow man.

III. The Race of Faith (7)

5:7 ¶ You ran well. Who hindered you from obeying the truth?

Here Paul likens the faith life to a race in which many runners compete. He commends the Galatians for running their race well. When was that? The first time Paul came to Galatia. We have seen in Acts 14 how the Galatians received Paul graciously, how they listened to him intently, how they were quickly born again, filled with the Spirit, set free from idolatry, liberated from their bondage to the law of sin and death to become new creatures in Christ Jesus. They began their Christian race well, but now it seems something has happened.

. . . Who did hinder you, that ye should not obey the truth?

The Greek word translated "hinder" is drawn from the ancient Greek foot-races. It refers to the action of one runner who cuts across the path of another, knocking him off his stride and slowing him down, perhaps even causing him to fall. In his analogy, Paul is saying to these people, "You began your race so well. Who has cut in front of you to trip you up?" Of course, we know the answer to that question. It is the legalistic Judaizers who have come in behind Paul, teaching their doctrine of strict observance of the law. Paul recognizes these teachings as a hindrance to the Galatians.

In Hebrews 12:1 we find a similar image:

¹ Therefore we also, since we are surrounded by so great a cloud of witnesses, let us lay aside every weight, and the sin which so easily ensnares us, and let us run with endurance the race that is set before us,

Again we see a picture of a runner who is weighed down with unnecessary encumbrances, causing him to falter and stumble. That weight is the weight of the law and does not set free, but like the sin it exposes, actually entangles itself about the feet to cause defeat and failure. That's why Paul warns the Galatians not to become entangled again with the yoke of bondage.

IV. Leaven of the Law (8–9)

5:8 This persuasion does not *come* from Him who calls you.

In other words, "It is not God who is cutting you off or persuading you to follow the law."

5:9 A little leaven leavens the whole lump.

Here Paul likens the law to leaven (yeast). Now in the Bible, leaven is never used to symbolize anything good. For example, in Mark 8:15 Jesus cautioned His disciples: "Take heed, beware of the leaven of the Pharisees, and of the leaven of Herod." The disciples didn't understand what He meant. They thought He was referring to actual bread, when what He was really speaking about was the teaching of the Pharisees.

This is precisely what Paul is referring to in verse 9. He is explaining that if the Galatians heed the leaven of the legalistic Judaizers, they will be led into error. A little bit of the law will obligate them to keep all of it, just as a little sin in a person's life will spread throughout his being and cause his downfall.

What is the answer to this problem? The solution is to purge the leaven out. It must be cast out, just as Ishmael and Hagar were cast out of Abraham's household. By allowing the leaven of Egypt into his household, Abraham brought disruption into his home. That leaven had to be purged before it affected the child of promise.

So it is in our lives today. The Spirit of God cannot cohabit with sin. That's why we must take heed, to beware the leaven of sin. We must also be on our guard against the leaven of the law that brought sin. To live a life truly pleasing to our Lord, we must avoid works of the law as carefully as we avoid works of iniquity. One gets us out of God's will; the other gets us out of His grace. Neither gets us any closer to righteousness.

V. The Offence of the Cross (10–11)

> **5:10 I have confidence in you, in the Lord, that you will have no other mind; but he who troubles you shall bear his judgment, whoever he is.**

Paul expresses confidence in the Galatians that they will see and understand what he is explaining to them, and fall back upon the foundation he had left in them before his departure. He is trusting they will realize the truth of his message of grace and remove the person (or persons) from their midst who is causing confusion and doubt.

> **5:11 ¶ And I, brethren, if I still preach circumcision, why do I still suffer persecution? Then the offense of the cross has ceased.**

Obviously, part of the confusion caused by the legalistic Judaizers is telling the gullible Galatians that Paul himself, being a Jew, believes in circumcision. This one point was enough to thoroughly disrupt the churches in Galatia and to throw them into a state of turmoil. If the great apostle Paul believes in and practices circumcision, then who were they to refuse to adhere to the practice? Paul is setting the record straight once and for all by pointing out to the Galatians that if he ascribes to the practice of circumcision as the Judaizers says he does, he would not still be persecuted by them and the proponents of Judaism.

. . . Then is the offence of the cross ceased.

Paul emphasizes that if he were trusting in circumcision and the keeping of the Jewish law for salvation, the cross of Jesus Christ would have no significance. If it was the Jewish law that saved men, then what would it matter whether another Jew had died on the cross at the hands of the Roman conquerors? The cross would be meaningless.

The "offence of the cross" to which Paul refers to is its simplicity: simplicity of salvation, simplicity of spirituality. Once people grasp the truth that the cross of Calvary paid fully for all their sins so God can now forgive those sins, clothe them in robes of righteousness, and grant them eternal and abundant life because of it, no more room remains for great involved intellectual or religious discussion or debate. That's what Paul meant when he wrote to the Corinthians: "But we preach Christ crucified, unto the Jews a stumblingblock, and unto the Greeks foolishness" (1 Corinthians 1:23).

The cross was a stumbling block to the Jews because it was too simple spiritually. To them salvation required keeping a huge and complicated system of rules and regulations. The cross was foolishness to the Greeks because it was too simple intellectually. As members of a highly cultured civilization and culture, what possible significance could there be to them in the crucifixion of some unknown Jewish carpenter from Nazareth?

That's why Paul made such efforts to keep his teaching simple, even though the truths he shared were tremendously profound. That's why he prayed the eyes of the understanding of those who heard the gospel would be opened. He knew people would never really be able to appreciate the simplicity and beauty of the gospel until they had once truly grasped the full significance of the message of salvation through the grace of God by faith in His Son who was crucified so every person on earth could be set free from the law of sin and death.

VI. Religion and Heathenism (12)

5:12 I could wish that those who trouble you would even cut themselves off!

In the *New King James Version*, this verse sounds reasonable. However, in Greek it is much stronger. In this verse Paul addressed the question of circumcision once and for all, expressing his viewpoint about it (and those who preach and require it) in very explicit terms. The *New American Standard Bible* translates Paul's statement this way: "Would that those who are troubling you would even mutilate themselves." The *New International Version* makes Paul's meaning even clearer: "As for those agitators, I wish they would go the whole way and emasculate themselves!"

But the truth is, what Paul really meant to express was this idea: "If those Jewish troublemakers think cutting off a little foreskin pleases God, then in order to fully please Him they ought to go all the way and cut off the whole male organ!"

Although this statement may seem crude and extremist to us in our modern and refined thinking, the Galatians understand Paul's meaning perfectly. So do the religious Jews at whom this statement is aimed. In one area of Galatia in the city of Pessinus, there flourished a heathen cult who worshipped Cybele. To the followers of this religion, the highest form of worship was self-mutilation. And the highest form of self-mutilation for a man was self-castration.

Paul is saying to the Galatian Christians, "If these teachers of the law really believe that cutting some part of the physical body pleases God, then why don't they carry that belief out to its logical conclusion and cut that part off entirely?"

Paul warns against the heathenistic practice of self-mutilation because it is an abomination before the Lord. He reasoned that the practice of circumcision for salvation or spirituality, carried to its logical extreme, does not bring a man closer to God; in fact, it is sin: "He that is wounded in the stones, or hath his privy member cut off, shall not enter into the congregation of the LORD" (Deuteronomy 23:1). That's why Paul speaks out so strongly against circumcision in Philippians 3:2: "Beware of dogs, beware of evil workers, beware of the concision [those who preach circumcision]." This warning is his message to believers throughout the New Testament.

This theme of attempting to reach God or to please Him through asceticism (self-denial or self-inflicted punishment) is one Paul deals with strongly in the book of Galatians. He wants these believers to understand that to practice asceticism is to become "religious." Religion is defined as man's efforts to please God. In that sense, the religious person is no different from a heathen; both attempt to reach God or to please Him by their own self-efforts.

Paul sees very clearly the foolishness of trying to substitute self-righteousness for the righteousness of God in Christ Jesus. True righteousness can never be earned or merited; it can be received only as a gift by the grace of God who bestows it freely upon those who simply ask for it in faith. Thus, the religious Jews who worked so diligently to be righteous missed it, while the "unreligious" Gentiles who did nothing but believe God, received His righteousness without doing anything for it. That is part of the mystery of the gospel.

After Paul lays the axe to the root of the tree of circumcision, he leaves the subject to move on to a more positive aspect of his message.

VII. Called unto Liberty (13)

5:13 ¶ For you, brethren, have been called to liberty; only do not *use* liberty as an opportunity for the flesh, but through love serve one another.

There are always those who will be afraid to teach the message of liberty because they fear it will lead people to live self-indulgent, sinful lives. That may happen to some degree. Out of every 100 Christians who are set free from bondage, there may be two or three who will take advantage of that freedom to serve their own selfish interests. Some few will give in to the desires of the flesh. But I would rather preach the message of love and liberty and see 98 percent of those set free go on to live fuller, happier, more devoted Christian lives, than I would deny them fullness and joy and service just because some people can't handle it. God forbid we ever let our own fear and doubt keep in bondage the very people for whom Christ gave His life that they might be set free.

I once heard a foreign missionary say he didn't preach the message of prosperity to his new converts. He was afraid once they began to prosper they wouldn't know how to handle the increase and would turn away from God. However, people are basically the same everywhere. If a believer is likely to turn away from his God the moment he gets a little ahead financially, then he never was much of a disciple to begin with. What loving parent would want to keep his child hungry and naked just to ensure the child stayed dependent on the parent? Such an attitude is not real love, because true, mature love is not possessive; on the contrary, it sets the object of its love free.

An old saying states, "What you love, set free. If it returns to you of its own accord, you will have it forever. If it does not return, you never had it to begin with." I believe God treats His children this way. He wants our love only if it is voluntarily given. If the only way He can have it is by keeping us in bondage, He never had our love in the first place.

. . . Only use not liberty for an occasion to the flesh. . .

Paul brings out this same idea in Romans 6:1 and 2, in which he wrote, "What shall we say then? Shall we continue in sin, that grace may abound? God forbid. How shall we, that are dead to sin, live any longer therein?"

Even though we are not under the law but under grace, that still does not mean we are free to indulge ourselves in sin. We may have the freedom of choice to engage in sin, but we are not free from the consequences of that sin.

. . . But by love serve one another.

The flesh always calls attention to itself, but love draws attention to others. Use your liberty to choose love, not the desires of the flesh. Selfishness demands its own desires be fulfilled; love seeks to fulfill first the desires of another. In fact, that is the definition of true love. Love is that force within a person causing him to desire someone else's welfare more than his own. Unless we can honestly say we desire the other person's happiness more than we desire our own, we shouldn't flippantly tell that person, "I love you," especially if that person is God. To love God is to desire His will be done more than we desire our own will be fulfilled.

To love others is to desire to see them blessed more than to see ourselves blessed. Obviously, the flesh cannot love like that. Nothing short of the Spirit of God Himself can empower us to truly love others, to desire their welfare more than our own: "Greater love hath no man than this, that a man lay down his life for his friends" (John 15:13).

We may not be called upon to give our lives for someone else, but we may well have opportunities to give part of our material possessions so someone else may benefit. That's when we must be led of the Spirit because our flesh will rebel. The flesh is not capable of such love because by its very nature it is self-centered.

Scientists tell us the drive for self-preservation is one of the strongest of the inborn human traits. It goes against the grain of our human nature, our flesh, to put others first, especially when it means we will suffer loss. That's why our natural human nature is never able to please God; it's too centered on self. The only way anyone can be freed from the selfish human nature is by receiving within him a new nature, a new spirit that is not self-centered but "other-centered." That spirit, if heeded, will lead the person in paths of righteousness and truth and blessing.

Learn to heed the Spirit within you. His counsel may not always seem logical, but that's because it's not based on human logic but on God's logic. When He says give away what you desperately need for yourself, don't be afraid to comply. It may not seem natural, but if it were the natural thing to do, it probably wouldn't be the God thing to do. "Give, and it shall be given unto you; good measure, pressed down, and shaken together, and running over" (Luke 6:38). God rewards obedience to His Spirit, *not* obedience to the law.

The Spirit of God is the nature of God. And what is God's nature? John, the beloved apostle, told us "God is love" (1 John 4:16). Therefore to be led of the Spirit of God is to be led by love, the force that puts the other person's welfare ahead of our own. Christians are under law; not under the Mosaic law, but the law of love. There is a difference between being under the Mosaic law and being under the law of love. Law is imposed from the outside, love impresses from the inside. Law compels; love impels. Law is what we do because we have no choice; love is what we must do because we do have a choice. Law is what our bodies are forced to obey; love is what our hearts won't allow us not to obey. Law binds us to service; love frees us for service.

This law of love becomes the central issue and the culmination of Paul's message from here to the end of the book.

VIII. Fulfilling the Law (14)

5:14 For all the law is fulfilled in one word, *even* **in this:** *"You shall love your neighbor as yourself."*

It is only natural that Paul ends his remarks by concentrating on love because love is the fulfillment of the law. In Romans 5:5, Paul tells us "the love of God is shed abroad in our hearts." In Romans 8:16 he says the Holy Spirit bears "witness with our spirit, that we are the children of God." If we are led of the Spirit of God, who is love, we will always be led in ways of love. If we walk in love, we will fulfill the law.

God gave the Mosaic law because the people under the old covenant didn't have the Holy Spirit to lead them from within as we do today. They had to have an outward, physical law to constrain them and guide their actions. Now that the Spirit of God Himself has come to take up residence within our bodies, why would we ever want or need to return to being led by an outside rule? That's why we are free of the law, not to do as we please, but to do as the Spirit pleases.

To follow the Spirit is to fulfill the law because the Spirit of love will always lead us in conformity to the law. God's Spirit will never lead us to commit murder, adultery, bear false witness, steal, or do any of those things forbidden under the old covenant. The Holy Spirit will never guide us into actions that are in disobedience to God or harmful to our neighbor, but only into those that please God and benefit our neighbor. Putting God's will ahead of our own, and desiring our neighbor's welfare more than our own welfare is love. That's why following the Spirit, walking in love, is the fulfillment of the whole of the law.

IX. Walk in the Spirit (15–18)

5:15 But if you bite and devour one another, beware lest you be consumed by one another!

What does a person bite with? The mouth. Paul is speaking here of sins of the tongue, gossiping and maligning. It's not necessary to be around other people to bite and devour them. All it takes is malicious talk. That talk can go on in their presence or out of it, at home or in church, around town or a thousand miles away. The result is the same. Biting and devouring always results in someone's being consumed. Bite an apple enough times and it will be gone.

I once heard a person say he had noticed no great man or woman of faith ever talked negatively about others. I believe there is a great deal of truth in that observation. Godly people don't speak evil of anyone, even if it's true. They know nothing kills faith faster than an uncontrolled tongue. Godly people speak faith and love. The reason they do so is because the two go together.

Galatians 5:6 says faith works by love. Christians who bite and devour one another will never be great men and women of faith. Paul noted in 1 Corinthians 13, even if we have the faith to move mountains, without love it profits us nothing. Our faith works not so much by how much Word we have in our talk, but in accordance to the amount of love we have in our walk.

If you have been guilty of biting and devouring other people, especially your brothers and sisters in Christ, it's not enough to change or confess your wrong to the Lord. In addition, there is something else you need to do. If you have openly gossiped about and maligned someone, you need to go to that person and make things right. Until you do that, your prayers will be hindered. Answers to prayer depend upon faith, and faith depends upon love. If you know someone "has ought against you," you will never have a truly successful prayer life or ministry until that hindrance has been forgiven and removed.

Verse 15 speaks of biting and devouring "one another," just as verses 13 and 14 speak of loving and serving "one another." Love serves one another, but biting and devouring consumes one another. Here is the principle: Love edifies, but hate demolishes. Love encourages, helps, and builds up; but sins of the tongue discourage, hinder, and destroy. In the past, we've had enough division and demolition in the church. Let's join hands and hearts with our brothers and sisters in Christ (despite their doctrines or creeds) and work together to build rather than destroy.

If we really want to win the world for Christ, let's learn to walk in love, especially with those "who are of the household of faith" (Galatians 6:10).

5:16 ¶ I say then: Walk in the Spirit, and you shall not fulfill the lust of the flesh.

What does that mean to walk in the Spirit? It means to be led of the Spirit of God who witnesses to our reborn human spirits. The Holy Spirit in our spirits will always lead us in line with God's will, which is His Word. If we are always led in line with God's will, we will always walk in love.

Some people seem to have trouble with this concept of following the leadership of the Holy Spirit within. They say they can never tell if it is God's Spirit or their own spirit they are listening to. That's no problem. It really doesn't make any difference whether the leading is coming directly from the Spirit of God or through the enlightened, reborn human spirit. The test is the same for both. Does the leading line up with the Word of God? If so, then follow it. If there is not a specific Scripture to test the leading, then does it bring peace and assurance? If not, then don't yield to that leading no matter how reasonable or attractive it may appear.

Never be afraid of following your own heart, in line with the Word of God. Since God now lives within you, you can trust your own spirit. It has been reborn, renewed in the likeness of God's Spirit. Your spirit will never lead you counter to the will and Word of God. It's only when you begin to listen to your flesh that you get into trouble.

5:17 For the flesh lusts against the Spirit, and the Spirit against the flesh; and these are contrary to one another, so that you do not do the things that you wish.

Abraham had no trouble in his home until he became involved with Hagar, the symbol of the flesh. As long as Hagar was kept on the level of a slave, everything was fine. But the moment she rose in position equal with Sarah, things began to go wrong. So it is with you. Your flesh is fine as long as you keep it on the level of a slave. But the moment you begin to comply with its desires, instead of forcing it to conform to yours, you are in trouble. To be led by the Spirit means keeping the flesh in its place.

5:18 But if you are led by the Spirit, you are not under the law.

Remember, the law is synonymous with the flesh. If you allow yourself to become subject to the law, your flesh, you begin to reap the harvest of the flesh. But if you subject yourself to the Spirit, you walk in the blessing of Abraham.

The flesh leads contrary to the will and Word of God because it leads by what you hear, see, taste, and feel from the outside world. The Spirit leads through an inner witness, by the intangible and eternal. That's why God doesn't lead His children by signs or fleeces or outward manifestations. These may be used by God to confirm His inward leading, but not as direct guidance. Those who are sons of God are those who are led of His Spirit. Although the Spirit may lead contrary to outward signs and circumstances, never be afraid to follow Him. For the paths of God are the paths of peace and truth and light. If you are led of the Spirit, you are not under law.

5:19–26 The Fruit of the Spirit

I. Walking in Love

In the last chapter we learned that walking in the Spirit fulfilled the law. We discovered walking in the law was bondage to an outside force, while the inner voice of the Spirit leads in love, which does not bind but sets at liberty.

In this chapter we will examine more closely this Spirit-walk. In Galatians 5:16 through 18, the first letter of the word *Spirit* is capitalized, making it appear that Paul was referring to the Holy Spirit, which he is in a sense. Actually the capitalization was added by the translators, since the Greek does not indicate whether this word is capitalized or not. *Spirit* then could be referring to the Holy Spirit of God, or it could be referring to our human spirits, as in the statement: "For the flesh lusteth against the (s)Spirit, and the (s)Spirit against the flesh: and these are contrary the one to the other: so that ye cannot do the things that ye would" (v. 17).

Whichever way we interpret this verse, Paul's point is the same: we can allow ourselves to be led by our flesh (which is our old man, sold to sin) or by our spirits (which are reborn in the image of God's Holy Spirit). The one we choose to follow will determine the direction our lives will take.

To walk in the Spirit (or by our spirits), is to walk in love. If we will listen to the dictates of our own reborn human spirits, we will walk in the Spirit of love and, therefore, will not fulfill the lust of the flesh. We will not need an outward law but will fulfill all righteousness because our spirits (quickened by the Holy Spirit) will never lead us into disobedience to God or in opposition to His desires and will.

It is not hard to walk in the spirit. You can do that while you drive the car, do housework, teach a class, or run a business. Walking in the spirit is not a mystical exercise in which a person falls into some sort of trance. Nor is it a feeling. Walking in the spirit is simply walking in constant fellowship and communion with the Spirit of God resident within us. It is walking in line with the Word of God, moment by moment.

II. Walking in the Flesh (19–21)

It is important we understand the list of the works of the flesh Paul gives here is not comprehensive. It does not include every possible work of the flesh. There is no such list available because no one could ever enumerate every way the fleshly nature can manifest itself. That's why Paul ended this list with the expression "and such like" (v. 21). However, this partial list is sufficient to instruct us in the types of things the flesh produces.

Note also these are works of the flesh. This word is plural, indicating there are many manifestations of the fleshly, carnal nature of man.

In addition to the works of the flesh, let's consider for a moment the wages those works earn. When you and I work in the physical sense, we earn a salary or wages. So it is in the spiritual sense. Works produce wages. We know from Romans 6:23 what those wages are: "For the wages of sin is death; but the gift of God is eternal life through Jesus Christ our Lord."

Walking by the flesh does result in a product. That product may seem pleasurable and appealing. In fact, it almost always does for a while. Even the Bible admits there is pleasure in sin for a season (Hebrews 11:25), but that pleasure is short-lived. On the other hand the psalmist says of God, "In thy presence is fulness of joy; at thy right hand there are pleasures for evermore" (Psalm 16:11). The product of the sin-filled life is temporal pleasure while the product of the Spirit-filled life is peace and joy.

The fruit of the Spirit keeps on producing long after the original seed is sown. What is sown to the flesh yields temporary results because being corruptible eventually goes back to corruption. That which is sown to the Spirit, being incorruptible seed, goes on producing forever. The two may appear indistinguishable for a while, just as Ishmael and Isaac may have looked alike in the natural realm. However, there was a difference between them, an internal difference. Ishmael was born of the fleshly desire, while Isaac was born of the promise of the Spirit. The natural race of Ishmael exists today, but it will pass away at the end of the age. The spiritual race of Isaac will never end but will go on forever after the flesh is gone.

A. Works of the Flesh

> **5:19–21 ¶ Now the works of the flesh are evident, which are: adultery, fornication, uncleanness, lewdness, 20 idolatry, sorcery, hatred, contentions, jealousies, outbursts of wrath, selfish ambitions, dissensions, heresies, 21 envy, murders, drunkenness, revelries, and the like; of which I tell you beforehand, just as I also told *you* in time past, that those who practice such things will not inherit the kingdom of God.**

1. Adultery

Whenever this word is used in the Bible, it usually refers to illicit sexual activity by a married individual with someone other than his or her spouse.

2. Fornication

This word is usually used to refer to illicit sexual activity by an unmarried person. So if an unmarried man had sex with a married woman, he would be guilty of fornication while she would be committing adultery. When two people who are married but not to each other engage in a sexual union, their relationship is adulterous. Two unmarried people who engage in sex would be guilty of fornication.

3. Uncleanness

This word deals more with the thought leading to the physical sex act rather than to the act itself. No sin, especially sexual sin, ever begins from the outside; rather it begins in the mind of the person who commits it. Uncleanness deals with evil sexual thoughts and desires. In this respect it could be translated as lust.

4. Lasciviousness

When unclean thoughts control the person, it is called lasciviousness. This causes a person to seek after sexual activity such as dirty magazines and movies. He mentally undresses women and has a cheap attitude toward sex. The lascivious person has given himself over to his sexual craving.

5. Idolatry

In the day in which these verses were written, idolatry referred to the worship of graven images. Today it includes giving preeminence to anything other than God. It could be money, power, position, fame, glory, even a business, club or amusement (such as a hobby, sport, or pastime). None of these things are evil in themselves, but they become evil when a person elevates that thing to a higher position than God. In that sense, we must constantly be on our guard against spiritual idolatry.

6. Witchcraft

This word is interesting. In the Greek it is *pharmakeia*, from which we derive our English word *pharmacy*. Witchcraft has always revolved around the use of drugs, as evidenced by the origin of this word. To us in our modern-day world, the word conjures up images of an old woman in a long black gown and tall hat flying through the air on a broomstick.

True witchcraft is no joking matter. It is not to be confused with innocent child's play. It is a multi-million-dollar business involving not only spiritists and the occult, but also a thriving drug culture threatening to destroy our way of life.

7. Hatred

Hatred is defined as personal hostility toward someone else. Like lust, it is a mental sin. A person can be smiling and cheerful on the outside and be seething with internal hatred. Sooner or later that emotion will find expression through words or deeds or by destroying the mind and body of the one who harbors it inside. Like all mental sins, hatred is a cancer. It harms the one it inhabits far more than the one to whom it is directed. That's why Christians are warned to put away all anger, wrath, and malice (Colossians 3:8). It's for our own good.

8. Variance

Variance simply means disagreement. It has to do with being at odds with people. The result is dislike between two people or two groups simply because of a difference in viewpoint. As Christians we are not required to agree on every issue of life, but we are warned against allowing our differences of opinion to lead to animosity, another of the mental sins with its attendant power to destroy the one who harbors it.

When we find ourselves in variance with someone, we are not to respond in kind. Whatever their attitude or action toward us, we are to respond in love. We cannot allow ourselves to become a party to anger, wrath, or malice, because if we do, we will reap the bitter fruit of our own wrong attitude.

9. Emulations

This is akin to jealousy but usually revolves around spiritual matters. In a sense, it is trying to play spiritual king of the mountain. It is an attitude that will not cooperate with others unless it gets its own way. We would call it ambition or rivalry.

10. Wrath

Wrath is the outward manifestation of inward hatred. It refers to emotional outbursts, explosions of anger.

11. Strife

Strife simply means discord or disharmony. These are musical terms relating to musicians playing together so their instruments or voices blend together as one. It is impossible for one person alone to be in discord or disharmony. To have discord or disharmony there must be more than one person involved. Strife is a group-related activity. It manifests itself in temper tantrums, complaining, and troublemaking, but its root source is lack of love. Just as darkness is the result of the absence of light, strife is the result of the absence of love.

As light always overcomes darkness, so love always overcomes strife. It is important to walk in love because it is the greatest power on earth. Nothing can stand against it. It will always be triumphant over evil and cover a multitude of sins.

12. Seditions

Seditions are factions or divisions over points other than personalities. What causes religious groups to split apart one from the other? Isn't it usually over some minor viewpoint rather than an individual? One person or group decides a specific doctrine or tradition must be kept at all costs. Unless it is done, they threaten to draw apart and dissolve their union with the rest of the group. That is sedition. It is spiritual treason.

13. Heresies

A heresy is an opinion contrary to the Word of God. Most heresies begin as seditions, group disruptions over a point of order or law. Eventually these disputes result in separation. One group holding to its opinion, splits away to follow its own interpretation. Many times this interpretation is in opposition to the Word of God. If so, it is heresy.

14. Envyings

Envy is jealousy without a particular target. It is also an inward or mental sin. It is the attitude that "everyone gets a better break than me." Whereas jealousy is directed toward one particular person, envy is toward all.

15. Murders

Notice, Paul did not say killing is wrong, but "murders." Murder is always condemned in the Word of God. The Bible is explicit in its condemnation of murder, which it defines in Proverbs 6:17 as the shedding of innocent blood. Therefore the Bible does condone capital punishment, or the shedding of guilty blood, which was instituted by God thousands of years before it became a political issue.

In Genesis 9:6 the Lord said to Noah and his family: "Whoso sheddeth man's blood, by man shall his blood be shed: for in the image of God made he man." This is the basis for capital punishment for murder. It also applies to the shedding of blood during times of warfare. Those who make war against others will have their own blood shed by their fellow man. No Christian should ever feel guilty for serving in the armed forces to defend his nation, even if it means shedding the blood of her enemies. God ordained for man to shed the blood of those who would take the lives of the innocent. That's why we have policemen who carry deadly weapons, not to murder, but to protect them against the evil that is loose in this world.

"But doesn't the Bible say, 'Thou shalt not kill?'" No, it says, "Thou shalt not murder." There is a difference. Confusion has arisen because of a mistranslation of the Hebrew word that means to take the life of an innocent person. The only time the word is correctly translated is when Jesus quoted this commandment to the rich young ruler, "Thou shalt do no murder" (Matthew 19:18). We read in Ecclesiastes 3:3 that there is "a time to kill, and a time to heal." The Bible does not contradict itself. When it says there is a time to kill, it is referring to the taking of life by legal means. When it says not to murder, it is referring to the taking of life by illegal means. One is justifiable; the other is not.

16. Drunkenness

The Word of God has always condemned drunkenness, which is the excessive use of alcohol.

17. Revellings

This simply refers to wild parties, carousing, and brawling which usually accompany drunkenness.

18. And Such Like

As we have noted, this is Paul's way of indicating the sins he has listed are not inclusive. Instead, it is a partial listing of the many manifestations of the flesh.

B. Why Should Saints Act like Sinners?

. . . Of the which I tell you before, as I have also told you in time past, that they which do such things shall not inherit the kingdom of God (v. 21).

Now we must be very careful in our interpretation of this verse or else we will destroy Paul's message to the Galatians. It would seem Paul is saying any believer who has envy or strife in his heart will not go to heaven. If so, we are all condemned, for who has not been guilty of at least one of these kinds of behavior or "such like"? Does this mean we will not inherit the kingdom of God?

No, God does not categorize sins. The concept of degree of sins is man's invention, not God's. He doesn't rank sins in order of their importance. In Romans 14:23, Paul tells us "whatsoever is not of faith is sin." Envy is sin and murder is sin. Jealousy is sin and adultery is sin. God views the sin of inward thought just as evil and sinful as those of outward action. Jesus said that to think evil is to commit murder. He said that to look upon a woman and lust after her is to commit adultery with her. We have our list of greater and lesser evils; God calls all evil "sin."

All outward sins begin as inward thoughts. If we can stop the inward thought, the outward deed will never take place. We need to see the evil of sin and God's hatred of it, whether it is a sin of thought or of deed.

It seems Paul is saying that if we are guilty of any of these sins, we will not inherit the kingdom of God. If God does not categorize sin, then we are all bound for hell. Which one of us has not had a thought of envy or jealousy? A closer look at this verse, however, will reveal its simplicity and true meaning.

. . . That they which do such things shall not inherit the kingdom of God.

The Greek word for "do" in verse 21 means to practice. Paul is saying those who practice sin will not inherit the kingdom of God. Unbelievers are being referred to in this verse, not believers.

The unbeliever has a different nature from that of the believer. Sin is his way of life. He may have a godly thought now and then, but it is not his usual attitude. He practices sin because sin is his nature.

The believer cannot practice sin. He may sin at times, but righteousness is his way of life. Despite his occasional failures, he practices godliness.

8 He who sins is of the devil, for the devil has sinned from the beginning. For this purpose the Son of God was manifested, that He might destroy the works of the devil. 9 Whoever has been born of God does not sin, for His seed remains in him; and he cannot sin, because he has been born of God. —1 John 3:8–9

Paul is saying, "Why are you Galatians looking and acting like those who will not inherit the kingdom of God? You are born of God but are acting like those who are of the devil. I have told you (believers) in the past that they (unbelievers) who do such things will not inherit the kingdom of God."

C. Carnal or Spiritual

For four chapters, Paul speaks to the Galatians about legalism versus true spirituality. Then beginning with chapter 5, he tells them to learn to listen to their reborn spirits rather than their flesh. He wants them to understand they were slaves to their unregenerated flesh before they were born again, and could not please God. But now that they are born again of His Spirit abiding within them, they should put away the flesh and its desires and habits; they should begin to live by the Spirit of life that does not practice sin but that, like Jesus, always does those things that please the Father (John 8:29).

In 1 Corinthians 3:1–3, Paul wrote these words:

> 1And I, brethren, could not speak to you as to spiritual people but as to carnal, as to babes in Christ. 2 I fed you with milk and not with solid food; for until now you were not able to receive it, and even now you are still not able; 3 for you are still carnal. For where there are envy, strife, and divisions among you, are you not carnal and behaving like mere men?

This passage sounds as though it had been written to the Galatians, especially since Paul calls them "carnal" and refers to their "envying, and strife, and divisions." In the last verse he said they were walking as men. The *Amplified* Bible says "mere. . .men." Paul points out that although these people are believers, they are behaving like unbelievers. Carnal believers look and act like unbelievers.

In Ephesians 5:1–7 Paul wrote to the church in Ephesus:

> 1 Therefore be imitators of God as dear children. 2 And walk in love, as Christ also has loved us and given Himself for us, an offering and a sacrifice to God for a sweet-smelling aroma. 3 But fornication and all uncleanness or covetousness, let it not even be named among you, as is fitting for saints; 4 neither filthiness, nor foolish talking, nor coarse jesting, which are not fitting, but rather giving of thanks. 5 For this you know, that no fornicator, unclean person, nor covetous man, who is an idolater, has any inheritance in the kingdom of Christ and God. 6 Let no one deceive you with empty words, for because of these things the wrath of God comes upon the sons of disobedience. 7 Therefore do not be partakers with them.

Again this sounds like Paul's message to the Galatians as he spoke of walking in love as opposed to fulfilling the desires of the flesh through fornication, and all uncleanness, or covetousness, filthiness, foolish talking, or jesting, emphasizing again that those who practice such things have no inheritance in the kingdom of God. Who are these whoremongers and unclean persons, these covetous men, these idolaters? Paul told us in verse 6: "the children of disobedience." In other words, these people are the children of their father, the devil, who "sinneth from the beginning" (1 John 3:8). Paul told the Corinthians the same thing he told the Galatians, they should have no part in such activity because they were not the children of the devil, but the children of God. As such, they should be "followers" (imitators) of their heavenly Father, not followers or imitators of the father of the children of disobedience.

Those who engage in sin, those who are the children of Satan, will spend eternity with their father in the place reserved for him and his angels. But those with the new nature, the children of God, have a different inheritance and destiny. They will spend eternity in heaven with their Father and Lord.

Between now and the time we get to heaven, we Christians still have the freedom of choice as to how we behave: as the children of God or as the children of disobedience. In other words, as spiritual people or as carnal people. Paul said those who become involved in the natural activities of the carnal are like babies. They need to grow up. Although they are believers, children of God, because of their immaturity they act like the children of disobedience.

In verse 14 of Ephesians 5, Paul wrote to those who are in this situation: "Wherefore he saith, Awake thou that sleepest, and arise from the dead, and Christ shall give thee light." The image presented here is one in which those who are out of fellowship with God appear to be dead, just like those who are dead in their sins. They aren't dead; they're only asleep, but to the world they seem to be dead. There appears to be no distinction between them and the children of disobedience.

Paul said God is calling such people to awake and to arise from their sleep. The Greek expression rendered "arise from the dead" actually means *to* arise from among the dead. That's the problem with the church today, too many of the children of God are asleep among the dead. If they will only awaken and arise, the Lord Jesus Christ will give them light. They will have renewed fellowship with Him and with their brothers and sisters in Christ, and His blood will cleanse them from all unrighteousness.

This is what the Galatians needed to do. Any sinner can live by the law, but he will not be any nearer to heaven. The Galatians didn't need to live like sinners. They needed to use the Spirit of God inside them and live like God in this world.

III. The Fruit of the Spirit (22–23)

In verses 19 through 21, Paul talked about the works of the flesh. Here in verses 22 and 23, we have contrasted the fruit of the Spirit. There are several differences between works and fruit. Flesh produces works. The Spirit produces fruit. Works are recompensed by a reward that comes at a definite stated moment, like a paycheck at the end of the week. On the other hand, fruit does not have a predetermined moment to appear.

The rewards for work come as soon as the work is completed. Fruit, since it is the product of a seed that must grow and develop through a long process, takes longer to materialize. Even when it makes its appearance, it must still remain attached to its support for a while before it is ready to be used to meet needs. Therefore, although sowing to the flesh and sowing to the Spirit both produce results eventually, the rewards of spiritual seed will many times manifest themselves later than those of the carnal seed. However, being spiritual, their fruit is much longer-lived than that of a carnal nature and has the ability to reproduce itself indefinitely.

Throughout human history, carnal man has been sowing seeds that have produced a harvest of sin and death. That process of sowing and reaping will go on until the end of the age. But the Spirit of God has also been sowing spiritual seed that has produced fruit. Sowing and reaping will also go on until the end of the age, but it won't end there. The end of time is just the beginning of the era of righteousness and peace on this earth called the millennium. This will be the thousand-year earthly reign of the Lord Jesus Christ, the Seed of Abraham. Jesus was sown thousands of years before He made His appearance in the days of Caesar Augustus. That Seed, has produced and will continue to produce millions of other seeds that will continue producing in ever-increasing numbers as the end draws near. One day Jesus will return in glory to redeem unto Himself His bride, the church.

The fruit of that seed was poured out upon all believers on the day of Pentecost. It had taken a long time in coming, but once it arrived it blossomed forth abundantly, spreading everywhere within a short while until it covered the whole earth. Although it seems the fruit was hidden for a time, today it is once again bursting forth into an abundant harvest around the world. We are living in the last days of that mighty harvest. The results of the harvest won't end here; they will live on throughout eternity. That's the difference between works and fruit. Fleshly works prosper for a season, but the fruit of the Spirit flourishes forever and ever.

This is not the fruit of the Holy Spirit but of the human spirit. Jesus is the Vine; we are the branches. Fruit does not grow on the vine; it grows on the branches. Jesus wants us to bear fruit. The Holy Spirit does not need love; He is love. We need love.

5:22–23 ¶ But the fruit of the Spirit is love, joy, peace, longsuffering, kindness, goodness, faithfulness, 23 gentleness, self-control. Against such there is no law.

But the fruit of the Spirit is love . . .

There is one final difference between works and fruit. Notice "works" (Galatians 5:19) is plural while "fruit" is singular. There is but one fruit of the Spirit. That fruit is love.

"But I thought there were nine fruits of the Spirit," you may say.

No, there's only one. All the other eight are manifestations of love. What was the one great commandment Jesus gave the Pharisee? "Thou shalt love the Lord thy God with all thy heart, and with all thy soul, and with all thy mind" (Matthew 22:36–37). Then He went on to say, "And the second [commandment] is like unto it [the first], Thou shalt love thy neighbour as thyself" (v. 39). The reason He gave for summarizing all the law into two commandments was that love fulfills the whole law. We saw in verse 14 , it is the Holy Spirit who sheds love abroad in our hearts. There is only one spiritual substance shed in the heart by the Spirit. The other eight qualities mentioned here are simply manifestations of the one great fruit of love.

As confirmation of this truth, let's look at what Paul had to say about this "more excellent way" (1 Corinthians 12:31) in the great love chapter, 1 Corinthians 13:

> 4 Love suffers long and is kind; love does not envy; love does not parade itself, is not puffed up; 5 does not behave rudely, does not seek its own, is not provoked, thinks no evil; 6 does not rejoice in iniquity, but rejoices in the truth; 7 bears all things, believes all things, hopes all things, endures all things. 8 Love never fails.

But whether there are prophecies, they will fail; whether there are tongues, they will cease; whether there is knowledge, it will vanish away. —1 Corinthians 13:4–8

It is interesting to note that every one of the other eight manifestations of the fruit of the Spirit can be found in this descriptive passage about love. If we are filled with the Spirit of God, we have within us the power to display all these attributes of our heavenly Father, who is Love. That power comes from the Holy Spirit, but the fruit is manifested in our reborn human spirits because we are the ones who need these qualities, not God. Let's look at these divine traits one by one.

A. Love

This word in Greek is *agape*, meaning divine love, the kind of selfless love God displayed toward us in His Son Jesus Christ. It is the product of a mature human spirit in tune with God's Holy Spirit. This God-type of love is directed toward our heavenly Father and toward our fellow man. Filled with this kind of divine love, we fulfill all the law because we love the Lord our God with all our hearts, souls, and minds, and we love our neighbor as ourselves. This is the primary fruit of the Spirit, the one from which all the others are derived.

B. Joy

This is not happiness, which is an outward expression of pleasure, a superficial emotion dependent upon our current situation or circumstances. Joy is a deep-seated sense of well-being no outside circumstance can alter. The joy of the Lord is our strength (Nehemiah 8:10).

Possessed with this divine strength, we can face the worst situations life can hand us, and though our outward faces may reflect the heartbreak or turmoil we are experiencing at the moment, deep within we are secure, knowing God has not left or forsaken us. It is this joy that sees us through those times such as the passing of loved ones. Although we miss them, we are comforted because we know they are not dead, but are being received into glory where one day we will meet them again.

Some people misunderstand joy. They know it's something Christians are supposed to have, so they try to work it up through some kind of activity, such as worship or praise or confession. The joy of the Lord is not produced by physical manifestations or verbal affirmations (as good and sincere as these may be). This joy is a deep, abiding assurance that, come what may, God is still on His throne and therefore we will emerge victorious from every fiery trial. It is closer to confidence than to exuberance. It's not something we work up; it's something we rest in.

C. Peace

Peace is inward stability when everything around us is falling apart. Like joy, it is a deep-seated assurance, a calm in the midst of the storms of life. The joy of the Lord allows us to sing at midnight while chained in prison with our feet in stocks. The peace of the Lord allows us to lie down and get a good night's sleep in the den of lions.

D. Longsuffering

This simply means patience, the kind of patient endurance that works hand in hand with faith so that we inherit the promises of God (Hebrews 6:12).

E. Kindness

This is kindness toward others. Translated "gentleness" in *King James Version*.

F. Goodness

Goodness refers to treating others in grace as Christ treats us.

G. Faithfulness

Although the King James Version translates this fruit as "faith," faithfulness is more accurate. It is possible to operate in faith and not in love, as Paul noted when he wrote, "And though I have all faith, so that I could remove mountains, and have not charity [love], I am nothing" (1 Corinthians 13:2). Faithfulness simply means dependability. Of all the traits listed here, this one is probably the most sought by God, and the one He rewards the most:

> 23 His lord said to him, 'Well done, good and faithful servant; you have been faithful over a few things, I will make you ruler over many things. Enter into the joy of your lord.' —Matthew 25:23

Notice also the joy of the Lord does not come from hand clapping and praise shouting, but as the result of faithfulness in carrying out His assigned tasks. Through praise and worship we can again find the joy and peace of the Lord. Praise and worship do not bring the fruit. God gives it to us at the new birth.

That's why we are exhorted not to grumble and complain but to be faithful in whatever the Lord has put before us to do. A faithful person is a humble person, one who accepts his assigned task and fulfills his calling with devotion and integrity. He knows that in due time the Lord will exalt him as he humbles himself under His mighty hand. When that promotion comes, it is a source of real joy, one that does not have to be manufactured, one that cannot be contained.

H. Gentleness

The *King James Version* translates "gentleness" as meekness. Some people tend to confuse this with *weakness*. Gentleness or meekness does not mean being a doormat for others to walk on. It simply means being teachable. A meek person is a teachable person. The Bible tells us to "receive with meekness the engrafted word" (James 1:21). That Word may sometimes come from a totally unsuspected source. After all, God is not limited to teaching us only through those with whom we agree on all points. The truth is the truth whatever its source. If we are meek, we will receive that truth as from the Lord. We will be teachable, even by those with whom we differ.

Jesus said the meek will inherit the earth (Matthew 5:5). We are told by the psalmist: "The meek will he guide in judgment: and the meek will he teach his way. . . . The meek shall eat and be satisfied. . . . The meek shall inherit the earth; and shall delight themselves in the abundance of peace" (Psalms 25:9, 22:26, 37:11).

What way does the Lord teach us so we may eat and be satisfied and delight ourselves in abundance? The way of peace. That's what a meek person is, a person of peace. He has no need to fight for what's rightfully his; he learns to receive it directly from the Lord's hand, just as his Master did.

I. Self-Control

This is self-control in all aspects of life. It is summarized by the rule, moderation in all things. This obviously does not refer to moderation in sin; it is the legitimate needs or pleasures of life that need to be controlled. Food and drink are fine, but overindulgence becomes a sin. Television, magazines, radio, and movies are fine, but they can become idols if given too much of our attention. We need to control our every need and desire in order to give God as much of our time as possible. "So teach us to number our days, that we may apply our hearts unto wisdom" (Psalm 90:12).

In Titus 2:11 and 12, Paul wrote "For the grace of God that bringeth salvation hath appeared to all men, teaching us that, denying ungodliness and worldly lusts, we should live soberly, righteously, and godly, in this present world." This word "soberly" refers to temperance in every aspect of life.

The passage in Galatians ends by telling us "against such there is no law" (v. 23). When we walk in the Spirit and produce its fruit, the law has no power over us. We fulfill it, not by keeping it, but by following the Spirit of God.

IV. Life in the Spirit (24–26)

5:24 ¶ And those *who are* Christ's have crucified the flesh with its passions and desires.

We have already seen in Galatians 2:20 that we were crucified with Christ so the life we now live in the flesh we live by the faith of the Son of God who loved us and gave Himself for us. Therefore, while we are free, we also have a responsibility to live our lives in accordance with the will and desire of God who loved us so much He gave His only begotten Son that we might have life in Him.

5:25 If we live in the Spirit, let us also walk in the Spirit.

When did we start living in the Spirit? At the time of the new birth. Since that time we should be daily walking in the Spirit. Paul is telling these Galatians, who did not seem to realize this truth, that *now* is the time for them to awaken to who they were in Christ Jesus and begin to allow the Spirit to bring their outer walk into conformity with their reborn inner natures. That's living life in the Spirit, the essence of Christianity.

5:26 Let us not become conceited, provoking one another, envying one another.

If we are now new creatures in Christ — the son of the living God who freely gives us all things to enjoy — there is no longer any need of our seeking after power or position to make us somebody in the eyes of others. Again, we do not need to act like unbelievers. Sinners seek power. We need to seek the kingdom.

We can now freely receive everything we need for righteous living directly from our loving heavenly Father. All we have to do is ask, remembering the words of our Lord Jesus that when we pray, we are to believe we receive and it will be ours. If this is true, none of us ever need to be jealous of others or to be envious of anything they have, whether material possessions, power, position, health, or any other good thing. As heirs of

God and joint heirs of Christ, all things are ours. Therefore, living life in the Spirit not only frees us from bondage to the law, it also frees us from bondage to our own selfish nature that causes us so much grief and pain.

6:1–18 Ministry of Restoration

I. Restoring in a Spirit of Meekness (1)

6:1 ¶ Brethren, if a man is overtaken in any trespass, you who *are* spiritual restore such a one in a spirit of gentleness, considering yourself lest you also be tempted.

Notice, Paul begins this last chapter by addressing the Galatians as "brethren." This is a title used in the New Testament only between fellow believers. In falling for the deception of the legalistic mentality, these people have fallen "short of the glory of God" (Romans 3:23 NIV). But by using the form of address, Paul indicates the Galatians are still members of the family of God. They may have failed, but it does not change their relationship with God, their heavenly Father.

. . . If a man be overtaken in a fault . . .

The Greek word for "fault" or "tresspass" here is *paraptoma*, which is sometimes translated as sin, but which *Strong's* defines as "a side-slip (lapse or deviation), i.e. (unintentional) error or (willful) transgression." This word differs from the usual Greek word used to express sin. That word is *harmartia*, which *Strong's* defines as an "offence." In the Greek it implies missing the mark, while *paraptoma* implies an unintentional blunder.

By the use of this word *paraptoma* to describe what the Galatians have done, Paul is saying they have unintentionally stumbled and fallen into error. Their action was a sin, in the sense that it is an offence against God because by it they missed the mark of His intention for them. Yet it was not as though they had deliberately and purposefully chosen to disobey Him or rebel against Him. They had simply blundered.

Most of these Galatians are completely unaware that by walking into the trap of legalism, they have missed the mark. They do not realized what they have done. As we saw in Galatians 3, they have been so foolish as to fall for this deception because they have been "hypnotized" by the shrewd Judaizers who havd taken advantage of their ignorance and gullibility.

. . . Ye which are spiritual, restore such an one . . .

The question arises in such cases: If a person has fallen into error like this, how can he be rescued from his error and restored to fellowship with God and his fellow believers? Many Christians have found themselves mired in something they know is wrong, but they don't know how to extricate themselves from it. What they need is someone who is spiritual enough to perceive their needs and concerned enough to show them, not so much where they missed the mark, but how to get back on track.

That's where you and I come in. As the sons of God, our calling and ministry is not so much to rescue those caught in sin as it is to warn others before they become trapped by it. Many times our fellow believers are suffering just as much from the wages of sin as the unbelievers. That's why Paul wants these people in Galatia to understand it is not their job to condemn those who have stumbled and fallen into error, but to be the instruments by which the Lord can reach out and restore them to fellowship. The church of Jesus Christ needs to learn it is here to redeem from debt, not to foreclose on it!

The Greek word translated "restore" in this verse means to reset a dislocated bone. Notice, the bone is not broken, but dislocated. This can be painful in our physical bodies and also in the body of Christ. We who are spiritual are to restore that person to the place of full usage in the body of Christ. Legalism puts him out of place. Love restores him.

Some Christians seem to think their failure and lack of fellowship with the Lord will not affect anyone but themselves. That's not so. As the bride of Christ, we are to our Lord what Eve was to Adam, bone of his bone and flesh of his flesh (Genesis 2:23). The psalmist said of the righteous man that the Lord "keepeth all his bones: not one of them is broken" (Psalm 34:20). Since Jesus is the personification of the righteous man, none of His bones were ever broken, in fulfillment of Scripture (John 19:36). Yet earlier David spoke prophetically of Jesus' suffering on the cross, saying, "all my bones are out of joint" (Psalm 22:14).

As "bones" of the body of Christ, we cannot be broken, but we can be out of joint. A bone out of joint is painful. Paul told us in 1 Corinthians 12:26, when one member of the body suffers, the whole body suffers with it. None of us should ever think that our suffering is ours alone, or that our failures or blunders do not have an effect upon other members of the body. That's why people of prominence in the body of Christ must be very careful of their words and actions because their mistakes can be costly not only to themselves but especially to the hundreds and thousands of people who look to them for spiritual leadership.

Sin, whether *paraptoma* (a blunder) or *harmartia* (an offence), affects our fellowship with our Father in heaven and our brothers and sisters here on earth. If it's not dealt with, it clogs the channel of communication and blessing between God and us and, consequently, between us and those to whom we are to minister. It is vitally important we keep ourselves as free from sin as possible, so that channel will remain free and clear of obstruction. As the saints of God, as those "which are spiritual," part of our ministry is the restoration of those of our number who have been "overtaken in a fault." In many ways, it is every bit as important to restore those who are saints as it is to make new ones.

. . . In the spirit of meekness; considering thyself, lest thou also be tempted.

Do you recognize this "spirit of meekness" as one of the manifestations of love, the fruit of the Spirit? We who are spiritual (full of the Spirit of God) are to demonstrate meekness in restoring those who have fallen. Why? We remember the words of Solomon who warned that a haughty spirit goes before a fall (Proverbs 16:18). We are meek (gentle) with others who have fallen because we know if we are haughty, we ourselves are liable to fall into temptation just as they have done. We also know none of the other fruit gifts will operate in our lives as long as we are out of fellowship with God because of a haughty spirit.

When we come across someone who has fallen, it is the easiest thing in the world to become prideful. The devil will tempt us into thinking how glad we are such a thing could never happen to us because of our great spirituality. But such a thought is evidence of pride. In a sense, when we think that way, we have already fallen; instead, we are to reject that thought and refuse to allow it to take root in our hearts.

To look down upon the fallen is to sit in judgment upon them. When we judge someone because he has sinned, we have just joined him in his fall by our sin of passing judgment. Actually, in that case, we are in worse shape than he is because while he's repenting and coming back to God we're looking down upon him in pride and thus separating ourselves from God. Among the sevens sins listed in Proverbs 6:16–19 as those God hates most, number one is a proud look. God does not like pride.

II. Sharing Burdens (2–5)

6:2 Bear one another's burdens, and so fulfill the law of Christ.

Now at first glance, verse 2 and verse 5 of this passage might seem to contradict each other. One says we are to bear each other's burdens and the other says each person is to bear his own burden. We will look at this more in detail when we consider verse 5. Right now let's see why we are to share in carrying each other's burdens.

. . . and so fulfil the law of Christ.

What law was Paul referring to when he spoke of burden-sharing as fulfilling "the law of Christ"? This is the law where we are to love our God with all our hearts, and love our neighbor as ourselves. If we truly love our neighbor as our selves, we not only refrain from doing him wrong, but we will also actively seek to do him good. Are we satisfied with just not hurting ourselves? Doesn't our self-love push us to much greater lengths, to see we are made happy? That's why we are told to bear each other's burdens. By helping our neighbor bear his load (because we love him as ourselves), we are bearing our own burden because when he became us, his burden became ours. No longer is there your burden and my burden; now there is only our burden.

6:3 For if anyone thinks himself to be something, when he is nothing, he deceives himself.

When we go to lift up someone who has fallen into sin, we must be careful not to think more highly of ourselves than we ought. We must remember we are always liable to fall just as he has. This attitude will keep us from thinking we're something when we're really nothing.

Paul does not say here that we are nothing. That would be a denial of his whole teaching throughout the New Testament. Every person is important to God. Each of us is somebody in God's eyes. We were important enough to Him, He sacrificed His own Son so we could live.

Paul does not mean we are to assume an attitude of self-depreciation. He simply means we are to avoid an attitude of self-exaltation. We are to keep ourselves from becoming self-righteous. Otherwise we will be in danger of pride, of thinking that we are the ones who lift up the poor from the dust and the needy out of the dunghill (Psalm 113:7).

Nowhere is humility needed more than in the process of restoring the fallen to fellowship with God because then there is a real danger of thinking we're doing it by our own power or because of our own righteousness.

A person who thinks this way deceives himself. It's bad enough to be deceived by Satan or by others, but it is more tragic to deceive yourself.

6:4 But let each one examine his own work, and then he will have rejoicing in himself alone, and not in another.

In the Old Testament, David said, "Examine me, O LORD, and prove me; try my reins and my heart" (Psalm 26:2). But in the New Testament, Paul says, "Let a man examine himself" (1 Corinthians 11:28), and "Examine yourselves, whether ye be in the faith" (2 Corinthians 13:5). The difference is the presence of the indwelling Holy Spirit to enlighten our reborn human spirit. Under the old covenant, God examined people from the outside. Under the new covenant, He has written His laws on our hearts. God now trusts us to examine ourselves on the inside in the light of the law of love.

Paul is telling the Galatians not to judge others by what they are able to do. Instead, they are to examine their own work. Then they could be happy about what they had done, not jealous or angry because of what someone has or has not accomplished.

In other words, while we are to examine our own selves, we are not to run around examining (judging) others. That's not our business; that's strictly between them and God.

6:5 For each one shall bear his own load.

For every man shall bear his own burden.

In the *King James Version*, this verse seems to contradict verse 2, which says we should bear one another's burdens. The reason they seem contradictory is because two different Greek words are translated "burden" here. In verse 2, the Greek word is *baros*, which means a heavy burden (-some), weight. In verse 5, the Greek word is *phortion*. According to *Strong's*, a *phortion* was an invoice or a bill of lading. In this sense, it figuratively represents a task or service, as well as an individual burden.

When Paul speaks in verse 2 of our carrying each other's *baros*, he is speaking of a large and burdensome weight, whereas in verse 5, when he says each one of us must carry his own *phortion*, he means we must carry out our own individually assigned task or service. The two are not synonymous. In one instance, we are called upon to help shoulder a weight that has become too heavy for one individual to bear by himself. This is the load of legalism brought on by the fault of sin. In the second, we are reminded not to shirk our own individual responsibility or duty. We help others come to the place of strength to carry their own *phortion* again. One case involves a joint effort, the other an individual effort. Both are part of our overall task as laborers together with Christ.

III. Sharing All Good Things (6)

6:6 ❡ Let him who is taught the word share in all good things with him who teaches.

Let him that is taught in the word communicate unto him that teacheth in all good things.

The word translated "communicate" in the *King James Version* is the Greek word *koinonia*, which is often used to indicate fellowship or community. It also has the connotation of communication between people or of distribution of something among them. It is in this sense Paul is using it in this verse. His meaning is brought out clearer in the *New American Standard Bible*: "And let the one who is taught the word share all good things with him who teaches."

As we proceed, we will see this idea of sharing "all good things" with those who "share the Word" establishes the theme of the next four verses. Paul is introducing the basic principle of sowing and reaping, which he develops further in verses 7 through 10.

The Galatians have been giving large sums of money and goods to the legalistic teachers. Now it is time they share these blessings with those who teach "good things" from God's Word.

Why does Paul suddenly switch from the subject of restoring to fellowship those who have fallen into sin to this topic of sharing finances and blessings? This is actually not a switch from one theme to another; it is the continuation and development of the one central theme of chapter 6: *koinonia*.

Paul is teaching the Galatians about community, the shared life. He wants them to understand that in Christ they are one with each other, that they share together one common faith, one common heritage, one common commandment. That's why he spoke of lifting up the brother who has fallen into sin, of bearing the burden too heavy for one brother to carry alone, of communicating the good things of life with the brother who communicates the Word to all.

He wants these people to realize they are not in this thing alone; it is all for one and one for all. He also wants them to know nothing they give to each other is ever really lost because God will make sure it is returned to them in multiplied abundance, so there will be plenty for all.

IV. Law or Principle? (7–8)

6:7 ¶ Do not be deceived, God is not mocked; for whatever a man sows, that he will also reap.

It is likely this issue of sharing has arisen because the legalistic Judaizers who came in behind Paul are draining the Galatians of their material goods, using them to finance the spread of their religion of the law. In fact, it is probably strict adherence to the Old Testament law of tithing causing the problem. Paul is writing the Galatians to free them from the letter of the law with its binding restrictions based on obligation and duty. He is writing to set them free through the principle of sowing and reaping, which releases from obligation but results in manifold blessings to the one who gives as well as to the one who receives.

The principle of tithing is far different from the law of tithing. Tithing was a part of the Old Testament law, but Paul is reminding the Galatians they are not under law, but grace. He wants them to understand giving was a definite part of the overall plan of God, but it was never intended to be an obligation or duty. Instead, it is to be the normal way of life for those whose spirits had been born anew by the Holy Spirit of God.

Like Abraham who had instituted it, tithing existed long before the law came into existence. The coming of the Holy Spirit freed those who are in Christ Jesus from the restrictions of the law that they might live in the fullness of the Spirit. The primary fruit of that Spirit is love.

The reason you and I tithe today is not because we are demanded to do so by law, but because we are moved to do so by love. The law came by Moses, but love was shed abroad in our hearts by the Holy Spirit. The law was carved in stone; it is external, cold, dead. The love of God is written on the heart; it is internal, warm, alive. The law demands, but grace gives. That's the principle Paul wanted the Galatians to understand.

. . . God is not mocked: for whatsoever a man soweth, that shall he also reap.

Traditionally this verse has been taught in connection to sin. For years it was used as a warning that we were not to delude ourselves into thinking we could get away with sinning. Because of such teaching we developed a kind of Big-Brother-is-watching complex. Verses like this one were a constant reminder to us to beware because sooner or later our sin would find us out. That is true, to a degree, but it is only the negative side of the principle of sowing and reaping.

An evil harvest occurs only when bad seed has been planted. There is another side to this story, one that only recently has begun to be publicized. That side says good seed produces a harvest of good, both for the one who sows and the one who reaps.

Part of the reason for the traditional negative interpretation of this verse is an attitude of mistrust. Pastors were reluctant to preach the complete message of liberty in Christ because they were afraid if their people knew they were free, there would be nothing to keep them in line. Verses like this were dug up as a sort of warning.

Whether true or not, it is not really the heart of Paul's message to the Galatians. What he is stressing here is not fear, but freedom from fear. He is underscoring his message of the shared life by assuring the Galatian believers they should never be afraid to give because God has established a principle of life that guarantees no one can ever give himself poor. This verse is not so much a warning about reaping the wages of sin as much as it is a promise of reaping the fruit of the Spirit.

The principle of sowing and reaping runs throughout the Bible. In Mark 4 Jesus taught a parable about the sower and the seed. When His disciples showed they didn't understand it, the Lord told them in essence, "If you don't understand this parable, you won't understand any of them" (v. 11). He was saying all teaching in the Word of God revolves around the sowing and reaping principle.

This principle is very simple: Whatever a person sows, he will reap. That's why Jesus taught the people of His day to be givers because what they gave would be returned to them, "good measure, pressed down, and shaken together" (Luke 6:38). He did not mean by this teaching, they were to give in order to receive; that would be self-centered rather than other-centered. Jesus' message was the same as Paul's: "Don't be afraid to give to those in need; you won't come up short. I can assure you there's plenty more where that came from!"

The seed-faith principle works to the degree we understand it is an assurance that sets us free to give, not an enticement to get us to give. That concept is as false as the teaching we give because the law requires us to. One is legalistic; the other is materialistic. The true principle of giving is love. The first is law-motivated, the second is profit-motivated, but the third is love-motivated. Paul wants these people to know which of these three motivations God rewards.

6:8 For he who sows to his flesh will of the flesh reap corruption, but he who sows to the Spirit will of the Spirit reap everlasting life.

Paul is telling the Galatians if they sow to the lusts and passions of their flesh, they will reap lust and passion. Giving in obedience to law and giving simply to get are both means of sowing to the flesh. The nature of flesh is like that of the ground. It will produce whatever is sown in it.

Since the flesh is destined for corruption, all it can produce is corruption; but the Spirit (or the spirit) is different. It is eternal, incorruptible. It too will reap whatever is sown in it. Therefore, we want to sow to our spirits because the product will remain throughout eternity. We will reap a bumper crop of good that will never see corruption. That's a crop worth investing in.

V. If We Faint Not (9)

6:9 And let us not grow weary while doing good, for in due season we shall reap if we do not lose heart.

There are two ways to guarantee crop failure when sowing spiritual seed. The first is to sow it unto the flesh. Since the flesh is carnal, it cannot reproduce spiritual seed. The second is to neglect the seed sown in spiritual ground. Once the seed is sown, it must be carefully tended. The ground must be cultivated, the seed watered, and the grass and weeds removed. All this is hard work, as any farmer can tell you. Living by the principle of sowing and reaping requires diligence, but it is well worth it when harvest time comes.

The seed sown in good ground will never produce a harvest if the sower faints because of the trials and frustrations brought on by the enemy who comes in to sow tares (weeds) among the wheat (good seed). The writer of Hebrews understood this truth when he warned "lest ye be wearied and faint in your minds" (Hebrews 12:3).

It is not in the spirit we are tempted to give up; it's always in our minds. It is there the battle takes place as the devil attacks in an effort to cause us to give up. We must remember we are never beaten until we decide we are beaten. As long as our minds are firmly set, the devil and his demons are powerless to prevent our seed from producing a harvest of fruit. The time to rejoice in that harvest is not when it is finally brought in, but while the seed is still in the ground. That's faith in action, faith that keeps us from digging up the seed before it has had a chance to reproduce.

VI. Do Good unto All Men (10)

> **6:10 Therefore, as we have opportunity, let us do good to all, especially to those who are of the household of faith.**

Paul teaches that, as Christians, we are to do good to everyone, but most of all to other believers. We are to love the world, even our enemy, but not like we love our brothers and sisters in Christ.

Paul wants the law put away along with all its fruit. When believers become legalistic, they become judges of one another instead of those who love and care. Now that the Galatians hear Paul's message, they need to treat each other as the Lord treats them. God loves the sinner but not like He loves His own children. We need to do the same. We love the sinner and want him to be born again, but we do not fellowship with him as we do with other believers.

VII. How Large a Letter (11)

> **6:11 ⸿ See with what large letters I have written to you with my own hand!**

From here to the end of the book, Paul is concluding his remarks and jumps quickly from one thought to another. This particular verse has been the subject of great debate in theological circles for many years. Those who hold to the theory that healing is not part of the atonement cite it to prove Paul himself was sick throughout his life and ministry. They point out here he admits to having to write in large letters, probably because he suffered from some serious eye disease. Others say the Greek word translated "letter" refers to the epistle itself not to the individual letters of it. Therefore, they say this verse indicates Paul had no such vision impairment.

The truth is, in Greek as in English, this word "letter" is used for both an alphabetical letter and an epistle, so it could be taken either way. However, it does seem more likely Paul is referring to the epistle than to the alphabetical letter because the Greek word is in the singular: "See what a large letter I have written" (KJV), not "See what large letters I have written" (NKJV).

It is possible, however, there is an even more logical explanation of Paul's meaning, especially when we note Galatians is not a large epistle compared to others (such as Romans or 1 and 2 Corinthians)? Could it be Paul had more to say than is recorded here in this one short letter? In many ancient manuscripts, the letter to the Galatians is followed by the letter to the Hebrews. Just as there has been a long debate about the meaning of this word "letter," there has also been a lengthy and inconclusive debate about whether Paul was the author of the book of Hebrews. Some hold it was written about the same time as Galatians. The reason Paul's authorship of Hebrews is questioned is because in all his other books he begins by identifying himself right off (as in Galatians 1:1: "Paul, an apostle"). Hebrews, however, begins immediately with teaching.

Yet the two books are parallel in many ways. Both speak to the same theme of the law in contrast to grace. In reading both epistles, I am led to wonder if perhaps Paul wrote them both at the same time, Galatians serving as the introduction to the book of Hebrews that followed. This would make the "large letter" Paul referred to. In this case, the first part of the letter would have been sent to the Gentile converts in Galatia who would have received it with enthusiasm and interest. The second part would have been sent out to converted Jews in Jerusalem among whom a letter from Paul might have met with much less enthusiastic acceptance. If so, this would explain Paul's not identifying his authorship. If these hypotheses are correct, they would lend support to the theory that what Paul is saying here in Galatians 6:11 is, "See what a long letter I have written to you people there in Galatia."

In any case, the claim that this verse proves Paul suffered a chronic eye disease is unfounded, as is the assertion that healing in the atonement is disproven by such isolated references. It is amazing to me how some will hang on to such vague scriptures to disprove something so plainly brought out in important passages of the Word of God. Physical healing is one of the major works of Jesus on the cross (cf. Psalm 103:3, Isaiah 53:3–5, 10; Matthew 8:17).

VIII. Glory only in the Cross (12–14)

A. Show in the Flesh

6:12 As many as desire to make a good showing in the flesh, these *would* compel you to be circumcised, only that they may not suffer persecution for the cross of Christ.

The meaning of this verse is made clearer in the *New International Version*, which reads, "Those who want to make a good impression outwardly are trying to compel you to be circumcised. The only reason they do this is to avoid being persecuted for the cross of Christ." This reminds us of Paul's statement in Galatians 5:11: "And I, brethren, if I yet preach circumcision, why do I yet suffer persecution? then is the offence of the cross ceased."

Paul is arguing that those preaching circumcision to the Galatians are doing so because they want to gain glory for themselves and avoid being persecuted for preaching the true gospel of the cross.

6:13 For not even those who are circumcised keep the law, but they desire to have you circumcised that they may boast in your flesh.

Paul points out the contradiction in the message these Jews are preaching. If the Galatians are required to be circumcised to keep the law, why don't their teachers keep the law themselves? In Acts 15, Peter made the statement to the church counsel in Jerusalem: "Now therefore why tempt ye God, to put a yoke upon the neck of the [Gentile] disciples, which neither our fathers nor we were able to bear?" (v. 10).

In other words, Paul is asking the Galatians, "Why do these Jews demand you Gentiles be circumcised and keep a law they themselves cannot keep?" Then he gives the answer: "that they may glory in your flesh." "They are just doing it because it makes them appear more zealous for God. It takes away attention from their own failings and calls attention to yours. They can't keep the law, but they can make themselves look righteous by subjecting other people to it. It's all for show. They just want to bring glory to themselves."

6:14 But God forbid that I should boast except in the cross of our Lord Jesus Christ, by whom the world has been crucified to me, and I to the world.

Paul knows better than to try and bring glory upon himself. Instead he places the glory where it rightfully belongs, on the one who gave His life that we might live. We should not glory in our faith, but only in the Author and Finisher of our faith. Nor should we glory in our salvation, but in the one who purchased that salvation for us with His own precious blood. David reminded us: "Salvation belongeth unto the LORD" (Psalm 3:8). After his sin with Bathsheba, David prayed to God: "Restore unto me the joy of thy salvation" (Psalm 51:12). We have been given His salvation.

Glorying in our prosperity or our health or our success is also wrong because none of these things were originally ours. We have simply received them as a free gift in the great exchange. Jesus gave us His riches and healing and righteousness in exchange for our poverty, sickness, and sin. We should say with Paul, "God forbid that I should glory in anything other than the cross of Jesus Christ!"

B. Dead to the World

. . . By whom the world is crucified unto me, and I unto the world.

Notice, there is a double crucifixion here. Paul says that the world was crucified to him, and he was crucified to it. As far as the world is concerned, you and I are dead. That's fine, as long as we remember that, like the flesh, the world, with its lusts and affections, is dead to us. The life we now live in the world we live to the glory of the one who loved us and gave Himself for us.

IX. A New Rule (15–16)

6:15 For in Christ Jesus neither circumcision nor uncircumcision avails anything, but a new creation.

Notice, it is only "in Christ Jesus" that circumcision avails nothing. There is a natural, physical benefit to be gained from circumcision of the flesh. But in Christ Jesus, in the spiritual realm, that outward physical change is of no consequence at all because God looks not at the flesh of a person but at the heart.

The *Living Bible* paraphrases this verse like this: "It doesn't make any difference now whether we have been circumcised or not; what counts is whether we really have been changed into new and different people." The thing that matters to God is the inside of a person, not the outside. The New Birth, the receiving of a new spirit within, becoming a new spiritual creature, walking in the Spirit (or spirit), is what really counts with God, not what is done in the flesh.

If no one is justified by acts of the flesh but by becoming a new creature in Christ, then it makes sense that no one is condemned by acts of the flesh. That's what Paul meant when he said now that we are new creatures in Christ, now that we walk not after the flesh but after the Spirit, there is no condemnation to us (Romans 8:1).

Once a person is born again, once he becomes a new spiritual creature, he is no longer under condemnation because he is no longer a subject of the kingdom of flesh but has become a citizen of the kingdom of the Spirit. Thus his new spiritual life has nothing to do with acts of the flesh. This explains what Paul was talking about when he said he was dead to the world and it to him. The world is carnal; the believer is spirit. The two have no connection: "For what fellowship hath righteousness with unrighteousness? and what communion hath light with darkness?" (2 Corinthians 6:14).

> **6:16 ¶ And as many as walk according to this rule, peace and mercy *be* upon them, and upon the Israel of God.**

So then we are under law, but not the Mosaic law (the law written in stone); we are under the law (the rule) of love, written in our hearts. When we live by this rule of the new life in Christ Jesus, we have peace and mercy ruling in our lives.

. . . Peace be on them, and mercy, and upon the Israel of God.

This expression the "Israel of God" refers to the born-again Jews. Even though Paul is the apostle to the Gentiles, he has never lost his burden and love for his fellow Jews, many of whom were born again, but who had no real understanding of who and what they now are in Christ Jesus. Wouldn't this blessing pronounced upon them by Paul serve as a marvelous introduction to the book of Hebrews, which goes into great detail to explain to Jew and Gentile alike who and what we all are in Him whom God has "appointed heir of all things" (Hebrews 1:2)?

X. No More Trouble (17)

> **6:17 ¶ From now on let no one trouble me, for I bear in my body the marks of the Lord Jesus.**

Who has been troubling Paul? The legalistic Judaizers. Religious people. They have persecuted him for years because he preaches the liberating gospel of Jesus Christ, the message you have been reading in these pages.

Paul is saying, "If you want to know what these religious Jews are really like, look at my body. I carry the marks of their persecution. I have been beaten, stoned, and persecuted for my stand of liberty. But I do not consider these marks of persecution, but marks for the Lord Jesus."

As strange as it may seem, religious people still oppose Paul's message. They just can't believe God will set people totally free to live by their own spirits. The reason they can't accept this truth is because they have no confidence in people. The reason they have no confidence in people is because they have none in themselves.

Neither does Paul, the author of this epistle: "For we are the circumcision, which worship God in the spirit, and rejoice in Christ Jesus, and have no confidence in the flesh" (Philippians 3:3.) Yet in chapter 1 of that same epistle he told the Philippians, "And having this confidence, I know that I shall abide and continue with you all for your furtherance and joy of faith" (v. 25). What confidence was it Paul had in these people? The answer is found in verse 6 of chapter 1: "Being confident of this very thing, that he which hath begun a good work in you will perform it until the day of Jesus Christ."

Now we see where our confidence lies, not in our flesh or our abilities. Our confidence to live free of outward rules and regulations lies solely and totally in Him who began the good work in us. It is He who will perform it — not us. That's why we can be liberated to live by the Spirit and why we can set others free to live by the Spirit. The reason we can live free is because we are crucified with Christ; nevertheless, we live; yet not we, but Christ lives in us: and the lives we now live in the flesh we live by the faith of the Son of God, who loved us, and gave Himself for us (Colossians 2:20). When we live that way, we do not frustrate the grace of God.

To live like this will bring upon us persecution. Religion will not stand idly by and allow us to live free or to set others at liberty so they can live free. Paul knows this. That's why he tells the Galatians to stand fast in the liberty wherein Christ had made them free (Galatians 5:1). He knows what we have learned: religion is the worst persecutor of the church that has ever existed. It has been the cause of more martyred saints than any other force in history. Yet it goes virtually unchallenged, even in our day, because it passes itself off as spiritual fervor.

Religion is not confined to the established orthodoxy; it can be found in every level of society, both within the church of Jesus Christ and without. Like sin, religion is not a physical action but a spiritual attitude. It is the attitude of the Pharisee who prayed, "Thank You, Lord, that I'm not like this poor sinner." It's also the attitude of James and John, Jesus' closest disciples, who wanted to call down fire and brimstone on those Samaritans who did not receive them as they thought they ought to be received. Religion is not the exclusive privilege of the theologians in their stained-glass cathedrals; it can be just as prevalent among revivalists in their traveling tents. A haughty spirit is not a restricted quality; anyone can have one. That's why we who oppose it the strongest must be the most careful of it, "lest [we] also be tempted" (Galatians 6:1).

Verse 18 is a benediction:

6:18 ❡ Brethren, the grace of our Lord Jesus Christ *be* with your spirit. Amen.

Reference Book List

Barclay, William, 1976. *New Testament Words*. Westminster: John Knox Press.

Jamison, Robert; Brown, David & Fausset, A.R., 1997. *A Commentary on the Old and New Testaments* (3 Volume Set). Peabody, MA: Hendrickson Publishers.

Strong, James H., 1980, 15th Edition. *Strong's Exhaustive Concordance of the Bible*. Nashville, TN: Abingdon Press.

Strong, James & Thayer, Joseph, 1995. *Thayers Greek-English Lexicon of the New Testament: Coded with Strong's Concordance Numbers*. Peabody, MA: Hendrickson Publishers.

Unger, Merrill, 1996. *Vine's Complete Expository Dictionary of Old and New Testament Words: With Topical Index*. Nashville, TN: Thomas Nelson.

Vincent, Marvin R., 1985, *Vincent Word Studies in the New Testament* (4 Volume Set). Peabody, MA: Hendrickson Publishers.

Wuest, Kenneth, 1980, Second Edition. *Word Studies from the Greek New Testament* (4 Volume Set). Grand Rapids, MI: William B. Eerdmans Publishing Company.

Zodhiates, Spiros, 1991. *The Complete Word Study New Testatment* (Word Study Series). Chatanooga, TN: AMG Publishers.

The writings of Arthur W. Pink.

The writings and audio recordings of Donald Grey Barnhouse.

Meet Bob Yandian

From 1980 to 2013, Bob Yandian was the pastor of Grace Church in his hometown of Tulsa, Oklahoma. After 33 years, he left the church to his son, Robb, with a strong and vibrant congregation. During those years, he raised up and sent out hundreds of ministers to churches and missions organizations in the United States and around the world. He has authored over thirty books and established a worldwide ministry to pastors and ministers.

He is widely acknowledged as one of the most knowledgeable Bible teachers of this generation. His practical insight and wisdom into the Word of God has helped countless people around the world to live successfully in every area of the daily Christian life.

Bob attended Southwestern College and is also a graduate of Trinity Bible College. He has served as both instructor and dean of instructors at Rhema Bible College in Broken Arrow, Oklahoma.

Bob has traveled extensively throughout the United States and internationally, taking his powerful and easy to apply teachings that bring stability and hope to hungry hearts everywhere. He is called "a pastor to pastors."

Bob and his wife, Loretta, have been married for over forty years, are parents of two married children, and have five grandchildren. Bob and Loretta Yandian reside in Tulsa, Oklahoma.

Contact Bob Yandian Ministries

Email: bym@bobyandian.com

Phone:

(918) 250-2207

Mailing Address:

Bob Yandian Ministries

PO Box 55236

Tulsa, OK 74155

www.bobyandian.com

Other Books by Bob Yandian

Calling and Separation
Decently and in Order
Faith's Destination
From Just Enough to Overflowing
God's Word to Pastors
How Deep Are the Stripes?
Leadership Secrets of David the King
Morning Moments
One Flesh
Proverbs
Spirit Controlled Life
The Bible and National Defense
Understanding End Times
Unlimited Partnership
What If the Best Is Yet to Come?
When God Is Silent
From *A New Testament Commentary* Series (sold individually or as a set):

> *Acts*
> *Colossians*
> *Ephesians*
> *Galatians*
> *James*
> *Philippians*

PRAYER OF SALVATION

God loves you — no matter who you are, no matter what your past. God loves you so much that He gave His one and only begotten Son for you. The Bible tells us that ". . . whoever believes in him shall not perish but have eternal life" (John 3:16 NIV). Jesus laid down His life and rose again so that we could spend eternity with Him and experience His absolute best on earth. If you would like to receive Jesus into your life, say the following prayer out loud and mean it in your heart.

Heavenly Father, I come to You admitting that I am a sinner. Right now, I choose to turn away from sin, and I ask You to cleanse me of all unrighteousness. I believe that Your Son, Jesus, died on the cross to take away my sins. I also believe that He rose again from the dead so that I might be forgiven of my sins and made righteous through faith in Him. I call upon the name of Jesus Christ to be the Savior and Lord of my life. Jesus, I choose to follow You and ask that You fill me with the power of the Holy Spirit. I declare that, right now, I am a child of God. I am free from sin and full of the righteousness of God. I am saved in Jesus's name. Amen.

If you prayed this prayer to receive Jesus Christ as your Savior for the first time, please contact us to receive a free book:

www.harrisonhouse.com
Harrison House
PO Box 35035
Tulsa, Oklahoma 74153

Connect with us on

f Facebook @ HarrisonHousePublishers

and ⦿ Instagram @ HarrisonHousePublishing

so you can stay up to date with news

about our books and our authors.

Visit us at **www.harrisonhouse.com**

for a complete product listing as well as

monthly specials for wholesale distribution.